CW00743143

Keto for Women over 50 2021

The Ultimate Beginner's Keto Diet Cookbook Guide for Seniors to Boost Your Immune System with Easy to Make and Delicious Ketogenic Recipes for Easy and Permanent Weight Loss. 21 Day Action Plan and Success Journal Included.

Author: Olivia Williams

Legal Notice:
Copyright 2020 by Olivia Williams - All rights reserved.

This document is geared towards providing exact and reliable information regarding the topic and issue covered. The publication is sold on the idea that the publisher is not required to render an accounting, officially permitted, or otherwise, qualified services. If advice is necessary, legal or professional, a practiced individual in the profession should be ordered.
From a Declaration of Principles which was accepted and approved equally by a Committee of the American Bar Association and a Committee of Publishers and Associations.

Legal Notes:
In no way is it legal to reproduce, duplicate, or transmit any part of this document by either electronic means or in printed format. Recording of this publication is strictly prohibited and any storage of this document is not allowed unless with written permission from the publisher. All rights reserved.
The information provided herein is stated to be truthful and consistent, in that any liability, in terms of inattention or otherwise, by any usage or abuse of any policies, processes, or directions contained within is the solitary and utter responsibility of the recipient reader. Under no circumstances will any legal responsibility or blame be held against the publisher for any reparation, damages, or monetary loss due to the information herein, either directly or indirectly. Respective authors own all copyrights not held by the publisher.

Disclaimer Notice:
The information herein is offered for informational purposes solely and is universal as so. The presentation of the information is without a contract or any type of guarantee assurance. Readers acknowledge that the author is not engaging in the rendering of legal, financial, medical or professional advice. Please consult a licensed professional before attempting any techniques outlined in this book.
By continuing with this book, readers agree that the author is under no circumstances responsible for any losses, indirect or direct, that are incurred as a result of the information presented in this document, including, but not limited to inaccuracies, omissions and errors.

The trademarks that are used are without any consent, and the publication of the trademark is without permission or backing by the trademark owner. All trademarks and brands within this book are for clarifying purposes only and are the owned by the owners themselves, not affiliated with this document.

The Keto Diet & How it is Different for Seniors

The Keto diet features a high-fat consumption, a medium protein consumption and an extremely low carbohydrate consumption. The human body can work either by burning glucose or fat for energy, the Ketogenic diet, based on a reduction in carb intake, lets the body use fat as the primary source of energy and puts it in a metabolic state, known as ketosis. This happens when either dietary fat or stored fat is broken down and the body begins to release molecules - ketones - that can be used for fuel.

Due to this, you don't need to consume glucose to feel energetic and healthy. By undertaking a journey on the Keto diet, you can replace carbohydrates with fat and protein and get a lot of benefits in your 50s. For example, it can help you decrease insulin and blood sugar levels, shed extra pounds and, moreover, power your brain. One more important thing: when insulin levels are stable, you always feel satiated because the insulin hormone doesn't need to alert the conscious brain that you're hungry.

However, as we age, we need foods that will give us adequate energy, and it is easily metabolized to reduce the chances of developing lifestyle diseases such as diabetes. The keto diet brings the body to ketosis the body will utilize the fats for energy. The reason for writing this book is for people over 50 years to make the right choice when it comes to diet. The book will help you understand various diets that will suit your age and rejuvenate your cells while preventing any kind of illnesses.

When you follow the ketogenic diet, you will be able to avoid cravings such as those of sugar and choose something healthier and one which will promote cell development. You will feel fitter, healthier, and sharper.

Pros and Cons of the Keto Diet for Seniors

As we age, our bodies and its nutritional needs change. A senior transitioning to keto diet would therefore benefit from a variety of perks associated with the keto diet.

Before we dive into what some of these benefits are, it is important to note that you should consider consulting a medical professional who is knowledgeable about your current medical conditions and needs to determine if the keto diet would be best for you before taking the plunge into the lifestyle.

Okay, now that you have received the green light from your doctor. Here are a few things you may benefit from when transitioning to a keto diet as a senior:

- Easier Weight Loss

The more we age, the harder it becomes to lose weight. This can be due to higher stress levels, slower metabolism rate and rapid loss of muscle. The keto diet offers the perfect solution by burning fat at a higher rate.

- Deeper & Longer Sleep

Many seniors suffer from a variety of sleep disorders including, but not limited to, sleep apnea, insomnia, sleepwalking, and restless leg syndrome. Eating the macros allotted on the keto diet will encourage the body to indulge in adenosine activity leaving the body more relaxed and creating favorable conditions for deeper and longer sleep, with less disturbances.

- Avoiding the Onset of Chronic Diseases

The Keto diet has been said to help reduce the risks for a variety of chronic diseases, including but not limited to, diabetes, Parkinson's Disease, cancer, cardiovascular diseases, mental disorders, multiple sclerosis, and fatty liver disease.

Cons/Disadvantages:

Although Keto dieting has been proven to have many health and weight-loss benefits, a sudden or abrupt transition can cause a few mild, short-term effects.

These include:

- **Constipation**

A common mistake that ketogenic dieters make is to forget about fiber when it comes to their daily carb intake. A negative effect of insufficient amounts of fiber is constipation, which can be avoided by eating more green vegetables. In addition to these veggies, it is important to drink lots of water to prevent or help treat constipation. If you still find trouble treating your constipation, you can use a mild over-the-counter laxative to get rid of your problem.

- **Headaches and Dizziness**

In the early stages of your ketogenic journey, you would have gotten rid of caffeine (in many cases, it can be later reincorporated) and sugar from your diet. Because of their commonly known addictive properties, they tend to lead to you experiencing withdrawal symptoms. Symptoms of this caliber, however, last for just a couple of days, with mild effects and thereafter, no addictive signs or symptoms (physical). Therefore, after the initial effects of addiction, you will no longer experience the sensation of sugar or coffee to stay alert.

- **Bad Breath**

On a keto diet, your body burns fat for energy release, a process we have been referring to as ketosis. As part of this process, ketones are released in your breath and urine, and acetone, a particular ketone, possesses a specific smell. While the smell of acetone isn't necessarily malodorous (like in the case of bad or smelly breath that is caused by halitosis), you may notice a fruity candy or sugary smell. If you find it unpleasant, you can just use parsley, fresh mint, breath spray, sugar-free gum, or mouthwash, any of which would do the trick.

- **Leg Cramps**

It is not unusual to have leg cramps when just starting the keto diet, especially with most instances occurring in the night time. Stemming from a lack of potassium, such cramps can be remedied by taking potassium-containing multivitamins. Whether or not you experience such side effects, the taking of multivitamins is encouraged to prevent deficiencies that may be caused by the diet's restrictions.

What Older Adults Should Know About Keto Diet

There's a whole lot that the ketogenic diet does to help you reach a healthy and balanced weight and stay there: restore insulin levels of sensitivity, build and maintain muscle mass, and lower inflammation. A woman who consumes way too many carbohydrates can jump start menopause signs. Let's have a look at how a ketogenic diet can aid with the signs and symptoms of this menopause.

You'll Get an Increase of Energy

Our bodies will experience widely known energy dips if we fuel them with mainly sugar and carbohydrates. Especially if you take in quick and refined sugars (think about store-bought muffins, cupcakes, crackers, bread, candy, etc.). Changes in blood glucose can be stopped by receiving a steady amount of sugar.

High blood glucose makes the body send insulin to the pancreas, which then begins to take care of the way in which muscular tissue and fat cells absorb sugar. The reaction to the consumption of carbs is a powerful release of insulin to make sure that body can effectively manage the transport of the new sugar. With blood sugar levels down, the body will signal that it requires more sugar. This means that you'll experience many energy lows and highs in one day. This produces a reduced energy level.

Regulating Levels of Insulin

By going on a ketogenic diet, women with PCOS (polycystic-over-the-air disorder) can help regulate their hormones. A research study on the effect of low-glycemic diets has shown this impact. PCOS triggers insulin sensitivity concerns, which can be helped by the insulin-reducing properties of low-glycemic carbohydrates.

Burning Fat

Menopause can trigger the metabolic process to change and reduce. One of the most common complaints of the menopause is an increase in body weight and abdominal fat. A lower level of estrogen typically causes weight gain.

A diet with little or no carbohydrates is very efficient for decreasing body fat. Additionally, ketosis reduces appetite by controlling the production of the 'cravings hormonal agent' called ghrelin. You are generally less hungry while in ketosis.

Say Goodbye to Hot Flashes

Nobody totally understands hot flashes and why they take place. Hormonal changes that impact the hypothalamus, most likely have something to do with this. The hypothalamus manages the body's temperature level. Changes in hormonal agents can also disrupt this thermostat. This ends up being more sensitive to modifications in body temperature levels.

Finally Sleep Throughout the Night

Thanks to a much steadier blood sugar level, you will improve rest while on a ketogenic diet. With even more balanced hormones and much fewer warm flashes, you will sleep better as well. Reduced stress and an enhanced well-being are 2 of the benefits of better sleep.

Ketones, the production of which is stimulated throughout a ketogenic diet, create a very potent source of energy for the mind. Scientists have demonstrated that ketones act to help the hypothalamus. The body will have the ability to manage its own temperature level better. The presence of ketones works to make your body's thermostat better.

Common Mistakes Seniors Often Make on Keto Diet

It's often said that wisdom comes with age, and though that is in fact true in certain aspects, that doesn't necessarily mean that you can't make a mistake. This is especially when starting something new like the Ketogenic diet. A lot of beginners, irrespective of age, make the same mistakes when following the low-carb diet. Check out the list of the top mistakes people often make and avoid them if you want to get brilliant results from such an effective diet.

Inadequate Fluid Intake

On a Keto diet, the body tries to burn more fat and that's why it needs to be well-hydrated. Remaining hydrated, not just as apart of the diet but should be done as a long-term lifestyle practice. Because the diet plan generally has a diuretic effect, which releases extra fluid, adding to a person's weight it is important to become a huge fan of water. Keep bottles of water around you to remind you to drink up. Also, it is advised that you drink a glass before mealtime, which, further, outside of the diet helps with portion control.

Dairy Over-Enrichment

Remember, moderation is the key for you. Of course, you may find that dairy products are great for the Keto dieting plan. They're ideal high-fat and low-carb sources. However, don't forget that some dairy products contain sugar and overeating them can destroy your dieting plan. Due to this, you need to calculate the dairy products' calories and pay attention to their nutrition labels.

Lack of Fat

When it comes to the Keto diet, it means not just a low-carb, but also high-fat intake. At least 75% of the calories you consume should be provided from animal fats, monounsaturated fats, and olive oil. In such a way, you can ensure normal hormone function and boost your metabolism.

Excess Protein Intake.

While on a Keto diet it is vital that you moderate the amount of protein that you consume. You want the body to utilize your fats for energy which therefore leaves the role of protein to solely help build your muscle mass. Consuming more protein than your body needs can result in your body converting it to glucose which can lead to a high blood sugar content in your body and the in the opposite direction of ketosis.

Not Bracing Yourself for 'Fat Adaptation'.

It can be a bit time-consuming for your body to get used to burning off fat instead of glucose for fuel. So, you should prepare yourself and your body as well to experience the 'Fat Adaptation' or 'Keto Flu'. During the first week and even the second one, you may feel more fatigued, aches, and muscle cramps. That's pretty normal when your body adapts to another dietary need.

Not Checking with Your Doctor Before Transitioning to the Diet

This is a mistake people make regardless of age but it becomes far more vital for us to consult a medical professional as we near and pass the age of 50. Your doctor has the right to know about every change in your life. And especially when it comes to nutritional changes. Talk to your doctor before including Keto products in your diet plan to make sure that this's a good idea for you and it won't harm your health.

Secrets of the Fittest Senior Citizens

As you get older, it gets harder for you to make decisions. But if you want to gain more energy and stay fit as you pass the 50-year mark, knowing the 'secrets' of the fittest senior citizens can definitely set you up for success.

Here are some of those 'secrets' that also pertain to the keto diet:

Maintain Moderate Protein Consumption

Here, 'moderate' means no less than 25 percent of calories. For example, if your weight is 70 kilos, you can eat about 100 grams of protein per day. You should know that consuming too much protein can stop ketosis because the body can turn excess protein into glucose.

Reduce Your Carb Intake to 20 Grams per Day

This is the crucial rule of the Keto diet because only if the carb levels are very-very low, can your body produce ketones. However, this rule doesn't refer to fiber that can be highly effective in stimulating ketone levels.

Consume More Healthy Fat

The essence of this diet is increasing fat intake. So, you add enough fat to your meals to feel full. Just try not to overeat and not to eat when you don't feel hungry.

Regularize Sleep Patterns

People over 50 should sleep 8-9 hours per night. Keep that in mind as sleep deprivation may cause slower ketosis.

Consider Intermittent Fasting

If you skip one or two meals during the day several times a week, this can also stimulate ketosis as well as speed up weight loss.

Incorporate Exercise Wherever Possible

Inserting any kind of physical activity when sticking to the Keto diet may also speed up ketosis. This is not a requirement. However, visiting a sports gym can have a positive effect not only on physical but also mental health.

Actually, the Keto diet isn't so unique and quite easy to do. However, for most older people, it can be rather challenging to adapt to it at first. According to studies, it commonly takes 21 days to make a new habit. That's why you should be patient if you want to reach your goal.

21 Day Action Plan

Let's explore a sample 21 Day Meal Plan using the recipes featured in this ultimate beginner's keto diet cookbook guide for seniors to boost your immune system with easy to make and delicious ketogenic recipes for easy and permanent weight loss.

There are 40 delicious recipes in the sections that follow so please feel free to mix and match recipes to suit your personal taste and scenarios.

Remember this meal plan is meant to be regarded for informational purposes only. Everybody is different as such their needs and speed of weight loss may differ. So be sure to speak to a medical professional to be sure this meal plan would be best for you.

Day	Breakfast	Lunch	Dinner	Dessert
1	Ham & Cheese Egg Cups	Surf & Turf Cakes	Salmon Bites	Coconut Cinnamon Bread
2	Mixed Seed Porridge Bowl	Garlic Butter Shrimp	Tofu Burgers	Blueberry Cheesecake Mousse
3	Mascarpone Smoothie	Seared-Tuna Shirataki Rice Bowls	Pork and Bell Pepper	Mini Keto Cream Donut
4	Tofu Frittata	Crunchy	Fried Crayfish	Coconut Chocolate

	Turkey Milanese	Tails	Ice Pops
5	Ham & Cheese Egg Cups	Surf & Turf Cakes	Salmon Bites	Macadamia Chocolate Chip Bread
6	Mascarpone Smoothie	Braised Chicken Wings with Kalamata Olives	Tofu Burgers	Mini Keto Cream Donut
7	Mixed Seed Porridge Bowl	Crayfish and Avocado Lettuce Cups	Pork and Bell Pepper	Blueberry Cheesecake Mousse
8	Tofu Frittata	Creamy Dill Tuna	Ham Wrapped Shrimp	Coconut Chocolate Ice Pops
9	Fluffy Cinnamon Roll Pancakes	Keto Lasagna	Salmon Bites	Macadamia Chocolate Chip Bread
10	Low Carb Breakfast Donuts	Seared-Tuna Shirataki Rice Bowls	Skirt Steak with Chimichurri Sauce	Coconut Cinnamon Bread

11	Pear Milkshake	Surf & Turf Cakes	Tofu Skillet	Blueberry Cheesecake Mousse
12	Ham & Cheese Egg Cups	Crunchy Turkey Milanese	Tofu Burgers	Keto Cinnamon Crunch
13	Tofu Frittata	Keto Lasagna	Salmon Bites	Cinnamon Bread
14	Mixed Seed Porridge Bowl	Garlic Butter Shrimp	Skirt Steak with Chimichurri Sauce	Macadamia Chocolate Chip Bread
15	Mascarpone Smoothie	Braised Chicken Wings with Kalamata Olives	Ham Wrapped Shrimp	Mini Keto Cream Donut
16	Low Carb Breakfast Donuts	Crayfish and Avocado Lettuce Cups	Fried Crayfish Tails	Coconut Cinnamon Bread
17	Fluffy Cinnamon Roll Pancakes	Crunchy Turkey Milanese	Pork and Bell Pepper	Macadamia Chocolate Chip Bread
18	Tofu Frittata	Braised	Tofu Burgers	Coconut Chocolate

		Chicken Wings with Kalamata Olives		Ice Pops
19	Ham & Cheese Egg Cups	Garlic Butter Shrimp	Fried Crayfish Tails	Mini Keto Cream Donut
20	Mixed Seed Porridge Bowl	Seared-Tuna Shirataki Rice Bowls	Pork and Bell Pepper	Blueberry Cheesecake Mousse
21	Mascarpone Smoothie	Surf & Turf Cakes	Tofu Burgers	Coconut Cinnamon Bread

Be mindful that as with any other diet, it is recommended that you strive to remain active throughout these 21 days, incorporating exercise wherever possible. Now that you know the plan for the next 21 days, let's track your goals and successes.

Success Journal

Documenting your achievements in the first few days of your Keto journey can help create lifelong trends and help you catapult your body into ketosis. The next few pages will offer you a safe space to journal for first 21 days.

Please note: You will need to recreate these charts in your journal if currently reading on an eBook reader.

Let's begin! Take a breath. You got this!

Keto Goals

What are the goals you would like to achieve in the first 21 days of your Keto journey?

1. _____

2. _____

3. _____

4. _____

5. _____

6. _____

7. _____

8. _____

9. _____

10. _____

11. _____

12. _____

13. _____

14. _____

15. _____

16. _____

17. _____

18. _____

19. _____

20. _____

21. _____

Were You Successful in These Goals?

Tracking goal fulfilment not only helps you to gain confidence in your journey but also helps you identify points in which you need to work on.

Shade in the circle for each day you were successful., You will need to recreate this chart in your journal.

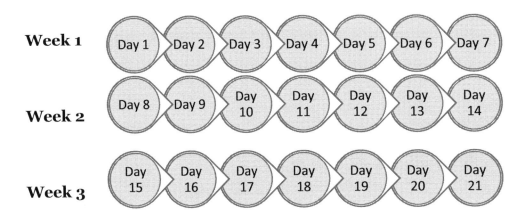

What Was Your Starting Point?

Let's get your starting measurements and weight., You will need to recreate this chart in your journal.

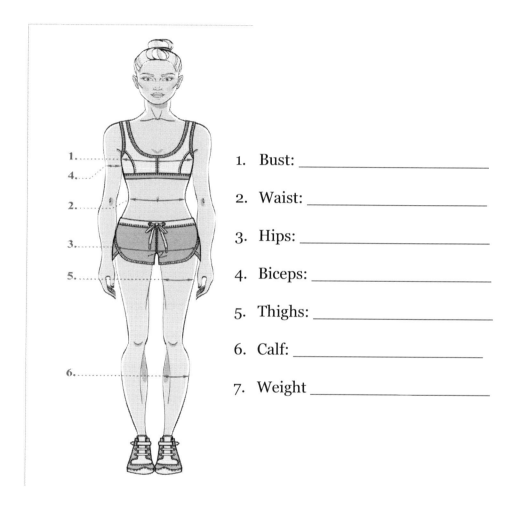

1. Bust: _____

2. Waist: _____

3. Hips: _____

4. Biceps: _____

5. Thighs: _____

6. Calf: _____

7. Weight _____

What Were Your Results?

Now that you have utilized the 21-day action plan, what are your ending measurements and weight on day 22? You will need to recreate this chart in your journal.

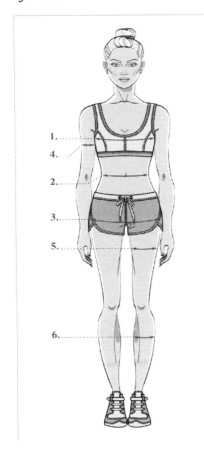

1. Bust: _____

2. Waist: _____

3. Hips: _____

4. Biceps: _____

5. Thighs: _____

6. Calf: _____

7. Weight _____

Congrats on completing your first 21 days! Now that you've got into the swing of things. Let's explore a few more delicious recipes to help keep you on track.

Breakfast

1. *Ham & Cheese Egg cups*

Serves: 12   **Prep Time: 5 mins**

Cook Time:15 mins

Calories: 101   **Carbs: 1g**

Protein: 8g   **Fats: 7g**

Ingredients:

- 12 Eggs
- ½ cup Frozen spinach
- 12 Ham strips
- 1/3 cup Cheddar cheese
- a pinch salt
- a pinch pepper

Directions:

1. Preheat your oven at 400 degrees Fahrenheit. Fry the ham strips until they are crispy and set aside.
2. Grease a muffin tray with oil and then place the fried ham strips inside. In a bowl, mix together the eggs and beat well.
3. Now add in the chopped spinach making sure it is dried properly. Pour the spinach and egg mixture in the muffin cases filling about ¾ of the muffin.
4. Now sprinkle over the cheddar cheese and the salt and pepper. Bake in a preheated oven for 15 minutes or until the cheese has melted. Enjoy!

2. *Mascarpone Smoothie*

Serves: 1   **Prep Time: 5 mins**

Cook Time:0 mins

Calories: 650   **Carbs: 4g**

Protein: 12g   **Fats: 64g**

Ingredients:

- 2 Egg yolks
- ½ cup Mascarpone cheese
- ¼ cup Water
- 4 Ice cubes
- 1 tablespoon Coconut oil
- ½ teaspoon Vanilla extract
- 3 drops Liquid stevia
- Whipped cream for topping

Directions:

1. Take a blender, and add in the egg yolks, mascarpone cheese, water, ice cubes, coconut oil, vanilla extract and the liquid stevia and blend.
2. Make sure that the ingredients are mixed well. Pour the mixture in to glasses. Top with whipped cream and enjoy!

3. *Blackberry Egg Muffin*

Serves: 4   **Prep Time: 10 mins**

Cook Time:15 mins

Calories: 144   **Carbs: 2g**

Protein: 9g   **Fats: 10g**

Ingredients:

- 5 Egg
- 1 tablespoon Butter
- 3 tablespoons Coconut flour
- 1 teaspoon Grated ginger
- ¼ teaspoon Vanilla
- 1/3 teaspoon Salt
- ½ Orange zest
- 1 teaspoon Chopped rosemary:
- ½ cup Fresh blackberries

Directions:

1. Preheat your oven at 350 degrees Fahrenheit. Take a blender, and add in the eggs, butter, coconut flour, grated ginger, vanilla, salt and the orange zest and blend properly.
2. Then add in the rosemary and blend. Pour the mixture in to muffin cups and then top each muffin with few blackberries.
3. Put the muffin tray to bake in the preheated oven for 15 minutes or until the eggs are set. Enjoy!

4. *Shredded Coconut Pancakes*

Serves: 2   **Prep Time: 10 mins**

Cook Time:8 mins

Calories: 575   **Carbs:4g**

Protein: 19g   **Fats: 51g**

Ingredients:

- 2 Eggs
- 2 oz Cream cheese
- 1 tablespoon Almond flour
- 1 teaspoon Cinnamon
- ½ tablespoon Erythritol
- a pinch Salt
- ¼ cup Shredded coconut
- 4 tablespoons Maple syrup

Directions:

1. Beat together the eggs in a bowl and then add in the cream cheese and the almond flour. Next add in the cinnamon, erythritol and the salt.
2. Mix properly and then pour some of the batter into a frying pan and fry the pancakes on both sides properly.
3. Put into a plate and sprinkle over the shredded coconut and then the maple syrup. Enjoy!

5. *Fluffy Cinnamon Roll Pancakes*

Serves: 4	**Prep Time: 20 mins**

Cook Time:6 mins

Calories: 125	**Carbs: 4g**
Protein: 17g	**Fats: 27g**

Ingredients:

- 2 scoops organic soy protein (vanilla flavor)
- 1 cup almond flour
- 1 tsp. glucomannan powder
- 2 tbsp. ground flaxseed
- 1½ cup water
- 1 tbsp. ground cinnamon
- 3 tbsp. olive oil
- 1 tsp. vanilla extract
- 1 tsp. baking powder

Directions:

1. Put the glucomannan powder and ground flaxseed into a medium-sized bowl with ½ cup of water and set aside for a couple of minutes.
2. In another medium-sized bowl, combine the soy protein, baking powder, and almond flour and set it aside, as well.

3. Mix the vanilla extract into the bowl with the soaked glucomannan powder and ground flaxseed. Slowly stir the remaining water into the first mixture and combine thoroughly.

4. Add the glucomannan mixture to the bowl with the flour mixture and stir well, making sure no lumps remain in the batter. Add in your cinnamon and lightly stir to create swirls. Put a medium-sized non-stick frying pan on the stove over medium heat and add the olive oil.

5. When the oil is warm, add a tablespoon of batter to the frying pan and spread it into a ¼-inch thick pancake. Cook the pancake for 3 minutes on each side. Repeat this process for the remaining 3 pancakes, or until all the batter is used.

6. Enjoy the pancakes right away. Alternatively, store the pancakes in an airtight container in the fridge, and consume within 3 days.

7. Store in the freezer for a maximum of 30 days and thaw at room temperature. Use a microwave or non-stick frying pan to reheat the pancakes before serving.

6. *Tofu Frittata*

Serves: 2   **Prep Time: 15 mins**

Cook Time: 40 mins

Calories: 347   **Carbs: 7g**

Protein: 22g   **Fats: 24g**

Ingredients:

- 1 (12 oz package) extra-firm tofu (drained)
- 1 tbsp. nutritional yeast
- ¼ cup coconut flour
- ½ cup full-fat coconut milk
- ½ tsp. glucomannan powder
- 1 tsp. curry powder
- ½ cup Button mushrooms (diced)
- ½ medium green onion (diced)
- ¼ cup black olives (seeded, chopped)

Directions:

1. Preheat the oven to 350°F and line a medium-sized casserole dish with parchment paper.
2. Put the tofu, nutritional yeast, coconut flour, coconut milk, glucomannan powder, and spices in a food processor and add salt and pepper to taste.
3. Process the ingredients into a smooth mixture and transfer the blended ingredients into the casserole dish.

4. Using a spoon, stir the diced mushrooms, green onion, and olives into the tofu mixture and flatten the surface.

5. Transfer the casserole dish to the oven.

6. Bake the tofu frittata for about 40 minutes, until the top of the frittata is golden brown

7. Take the casserole dish out of the oven and set it aside for about 5 minutes to cool down.

8. Slice into squares, serve and enjoy!

9. Alternatively, store the tofu frittata in an airtight container in the fridge and consume within 3 days.

10. Store in the freezer for a maximum of 30 days and thaw at room temperature. Use a microwave or small frying pan to reheat the frittata before serving.

7. *Bulletproof Protein Milkshake*

Serves: 2   **Prep Time: 15 mins**

Cook Time:0 mins

Calories: 448   **Carbs: 5g**

Protein: 16g   **Fats: 40g**

Ingredients:

- 4 tbsp. chia seeds
- ½ cup water
- 1 medium Hass avocado (pitted, peeled)
- 1 scoop organic soy protein (chocolate flavor)
- 1 cup full-fat coconut milk
- 2 tsp. vanilla extract
- Pinch of Himalayan salt
- 4 ice cubes

Directions:

1. Put the chia seeds and water in a blender and allow the seeds to soak at least 10 minutes.
2. Add all remaining ingredients to the blender and blend for about 1 minute, or until the shake reaches the desired consistency.
3. Transfer the shake to two large cups or shakers and enjoy! Alternatively, store the smoothie in an airtight container or canning jar in the fridge, and consume within 2 days.
4. Store for a maximum of 30 days in the freezer and thaw at room temperature before serving.

8. *Pear Milkshake*

Serves: 1 **Prep Time: 5 mins**

Cook Time: 0 mins

Calories: 398 **Carbs: 5g**

Protein: 29g **Fats: 28g**

Ingredients:

- 1 tsp. freeze-dried pear powder
- 1 medium Hass avocado (peeled, pitted, and halved)
- 2 cups unsweetened almond milk
- 1 scoop organic soy protein (vanilla flavor)
- ½ tsp. cinnamon
- 4-6 drops stevia sweetener
- 2 ice cubes

Directions:

1. Add all the required ingredients to a blender, including the optional ice cubes if desired, and blend for 1 minute.
2. Transfer to a large cup or shaker and enjoy!
3. Alternatively, store the smoothie in an airtight container or a mason jar, keep it in the fridge, and consume within 3 days.
4. Store for a maximum of 30 days in the freezer and thaw at room temperature.

9. *Low Carb Breakfast Donuts*

Serves: 6   **Prep Time: 1hr. 5 mins**

Cook Time: 25 mins

Calories: 145   **Carbs: 1g**

Protein: 11g   **Fats: 10g**

Ingredients:

- 1 cup unsweetened almond milk
- 2 tbsp. coconut oil
- ½ cup organic soy protein (chocolate flavor)
- ½ cup almond flour
- 1 tsp. glucomannan powder
- 2 tbsp. cocoa powder
- ½ tsp. vanilla extract
- ¼ tsp. stevia powder

Directions:

1. Preheat the oven to 350°F and use the coconut oil to grease a donut pan for 6 donuts.
2. Put all ingredients in a medium-sized bowl and use a mixer to combine into a thick batter. Alternatively, a food processor can be used.
3. Divide the batter into the 6 donut forms, ensuring all are evenly filled.
4. Put the donut pan in the oven and bake the donuts for about 25 minutes, until the top of each donut has browned and a fork comes out clean.
5. Take the donut pan out of the oven and set it aside for about 30 minutes, allowing the donuts to firm up and cool down.
6. Serve the donuts as a guilt-free snack and enjoy!

10. *Mixed Seed Porridge Bowl*

Serves: 1   **Prep Time: 15 mins**

Cook Time:5 mins

Calories: 302   **Carbs: 5g**

Protein: 13g   **Fats: 25g**

Ingredients:

- 2 tbsp. hemp seeds
- 2 tbsp. pumpkin seeds
- 1 tbsp. ground flaxseed
- 1 cup unsweetened almond milk
- 1 tbsp. lemon juice
- 6 drops stevia
- 1 tbsp. coconut flakes
- Optional: ¼ tsp. cinnamon

Directions:

1. Heat the almond milk in a medium-sized saucepan until it's almost boiling.
2. Turn off the heat, add all the remaining ingredients, and stir thoroughly. Note that, if desired, the optional cinnamon can either be incorporated or saved as a topping ingredient.
3. Set the saucepan aside for about 5 minutes to let the mixture cool down.
4. Serve the porridge cooled or still warm in a bowl and enjoy!
5. Alternatively, store the porridge in an airtight container in the fridge and consume within 3 days.
6. Store in the freezer for a maximum of 30 days and thaw at room temperature before serving. Microwave for up to a minute for a warm porridge bowl.

11. English Scrambled Eggs

Serves: 4   **Prep Time: 5 mins**

Cook Time: 10 mins

Calories: 239   **Carbs: 2.38g**

Protein: 13.92g   **Fats: 19.32g**

Ingredients:

- 6 large eggs, lightly beaten
- 2 Jalapeños, pickled, chopped finely
- 1 Tomato, diced
- 3 oz. Cheese, shredded
- 2 tbsp. Butter, for frying
- 8 tbs. Full Cream Milk

Directions:

1. Set a large skillet with butter over medium heat and allow to melt.
2. Add tomatoes, jalapeños and green onions then cook, while stirring, until fragrant, about 3 minutes.
3. Whisk together the egg and full cream then add the egg mixture, and continue to cook, while stirring, until almost set, about 2 minutes. Add cheese, and season to taste.
4. Continue cooking until the cheese melts, about another minute. Serve, and enjoy.

12. *Spinach Quiche*

Serves: 4 **Prep Time: 15 mins**

Cook Time:18 mins

Calories: 249 **Carbs: 9.4g**

Protein: 11.3g **Fats: 19.1g**

Ingredients:

- 6 oz. Celery stalk, chopped
- 2 cup Spinach
- 5 Eggs
- ½ cup Almond flour
- 1 teaspoon Olive oil
- 1 tablespoon Butter
- 1 teaspoon Salt
- ¼ cup Double cream,
- 1 teaspoon Ground black pepper

Directions:

1. Chop the spinach and combine it with the chopped celery stalk in the big bowl.
2. Beat the egg in the separate bowl and whisk them.
3. Combine the whisked eggs with the almond flour, butter, salt, double cream, and ground black pepper. Whisk it.
4. Preheat the air fryer to 360 F.
5. Spray the air fryer basket tray with the olive oil inside.
6. Then add the spinach-fennel mixture and pour the whisked egg mixture.
7. Cook the quiche for 18 minutes. When the time is over – let the quiche chill little.
8. Then remove it from the air fryer and slice into the servings. Enjoy!

13. *Parmesan Egg Muffins*

Serves: 6 **Prep Time: 10 mins**

Cook Time: 20 mins

Calories: 144 **Carbs: 1.43g**

Protein: 8.02g **Fats: 11.9g**☐

Ingredients:

- 4 large Eggs
- 2 tbsp. Greek yogurt, full fat
- 3 tbsp. Almond flour
- ¼ tsp. Baking powder
- 1½ cup Parmesan cheese, shredded

Directions:

1. Set your oven to preheat to 375 degrees F.
2. Add yogurt, and eggs to a medium bowl, season with salt, and pepper, then whisk to combine. Add your baking powder, and flour, then mix to form a smooth batter.
3. Finally, add your cheese, and fold to combine. Pour your mixture evenly into 6 silicone muffin cups and set to bake in your preheated oven.
4. Allow to bake until your eggs are fully set, and lightly golden on top, about 20 minutes, turning the tray at the halfway point.
5. Allow muffins to cool on a cooling rack then serve. Enjoy!

15. *Coconut Flour Bok Choy Casserole*

Serves: 6   **Prep Time: 30 mins**

Cook Time: 30 mins

Calories: 175.6   **Carbs: 2.4g**

Protein: 17.7g   **Fats: 10.3g**

Ingredients:

- 8 Eggs
- ¾ Cup Unsweetened almond milk
- 5 Ounces Fresh spinach, chopped
- 6 Ounces Bok choy, chopped
- 1 Cup Parmesan, grated
- 3 Minced Garlic cloves
- 1 tsp Salt
- ½ tsp Pepper
- ¾ Cup Coconut flour
- 1 tbsp Baking powder

Directions:

1. Preheat your air fryer to a temperature of about 375° F. Grease your air fryer pan with cooking spray.
2. Whisk the eggs with the almond milk, the spinach, the bok choy, ½ cup of parmesan cheese. Add the garlic, the salt and the pepper.
3. Add the coconut flour and baking powder and whisk until very well combined.
4. Spread mixture into your air fryer pan and sprinkle the remaining quantity of cheese over it.
5. Place the baking pan in the air fryer and lock the air fryer and set the timer to about 30 minutes.

6. When the timer beeps; turn off your Air Fryer. Remove the baking pan from the air fryer and sprinkle with the chopped basil. Slice your dish; then serve and enjoy it!

16. *Parmesan Omelette*

Serves: 2   **Prep Time: 10 mins**

Cook Time: 10 mins

Calories: 423   **Carbs: 6.81g**

Protein: 43.08g   Fats: 60.44g

Ingredients:

- 6 Eggs, beaten
- 2 tbsp. Olive oil
- 3 ½ oz. Tomatoes, cherry, halved
- 1 tbsp. Basil, dried
- 5 1/3 oz. Parmesan cheese, diced

Directions:

1. Whisk basil into eggs, and lightly season.
2. Set a large skillet with oil over medium heat and allow to get hot. Once hot, add tomatoes and cook while stirring.
3. Top with egg and continue cooking until the tops have started to firm up.
4. Add cheese, switch your heat to low, and allow to set fully set before serving. Enjoy!

17. *Egg Filled Avocado*

Serves: 4   **Prep Time: 15 mins**

Cook Time: 15 mins

Calories: 223   **Carbs: 4g**

Protein: 8g   **Fats: 12.6g**

Ingredients:

- 3 Halved Avocados
- 6 Eggs
- 1 tsp Garlic powder
- ½ tsp Sea salt
- ¼ tsp Black pepper
- ¼ cup Parmesan cheese, shredded

Directions:

1. Preheat your air fryer at a temperature of about 350°F.
2. Take 3 medium avocados; then cut it into halves. Scoop out about one third of the meat from each of the avocados.
3. Put the avocado halves in the air fryer pan with the face up.
4. Sprinkle the avocado with 1 pinch of salt and 1 pinch of pepper.
5. Sprinkle with the garlic powder and crack each of the eggs in the avocado halves.
6. Place the Air Fryer pan in your air fryer basket and lock the lid.
7. Set the timer for about 13 to 15 minutes.
8. When the timer beeps; turn off your Air Fryer.
9. Serve and enjoy your breakfast!

18. *Almond Pancakes*

Serves: 4   **Prep Time: 5 mins**

Cook Time: 20 mins

Calories: 302   **Carbs: 2.69g**

Protein: 14.52g   **Fats: 25.87g**

Ingredients:

- 4 Eggs
- 7 oz. Cottage cheese
- 1 tbsp. Almond Flour
- 2 oz. Butter,

Directions:

1. Add all your ingredients except butter, to a medium bowl, stir to combine then set aside to expand for about 5 minutes.
2. Set a skillet with oil over medium heat and allow to melt.
3. Add batter to the hot pan in batches and allow to fry until lightly golden on each side, about 4 minutes per side.
4. Serve with berries or whipped cream.

19. *Strawberries & Cream*

Serves: 1   **Prep Time: 2 mins**

Cook Time: 0 mins

Calories: 426   **Carbs: 12.87g**

Protein: 4.74g   **Fats: 41.79g**

Ingredients:

- 1/2 cup Coconut cream
- 2 oz. Strawberries
- 1 tsp. Vanilla extract

Directions:

1. Add coconut cream, and vanilla Ingredients to a blender then process until thick and smooth.
2. Transfer to a serving bowl, top with strawberries, and serve.

☐

☐

20. *Fennel Brown Hash*

Serves: 2   **Prep Time: 10 mins**

Cook Time: 20 mins

Calories: 290   **Carbs: 15g**

Protein: 20g   **Fats: 23g**

Ingredients:
- 1 small onion, sliced
- 6 to 8 medium Mushrooms, sliced
- 2 Cups Ground beef
- 1 Pinch Salt
- 1 Pinch Ground black pepper
- ½ tsp Smoked paprika
- 2 Eggs, lightly beaten
- 1 Small Avocado, diced
- 10 oz Fennel, chopped

Directions:
1. Preheat your air fryer to a temperature of about 350° F.
2. Spray your air fryer pan with a little bit of melted coconut oil.
3. Add the onions, the mushrooms, the salt and the pepper to the pan.
4. Add in the ground beef, smoked paprika and fennel. Crack in the eggs.
5. Gently whisk your mixture; then place the pan in your Air Fryer and lock the lid.
6. Set the timer to about 18 to 20 minutes and the temperature to about 375° F.
7. When the timer beeps; turn off your Air Fryer; then remove the pan from the Air Fryer.
8. Serve and enjoy your breakfast with chopped parsley and diced avocado!

☐

21. Almond Crepes

Serves: 2   **Prep Time: 5 mins**

Cook Time: 10 mins

Calories: 263   **Carbs: 3.05g**

Protein: 12.24g   **Fats: 22.73g**

Ingredients:

- 4 Eggs
- ¼ cup Almond milk, unsweetened
- 1 tbsp. Almond flour
- ¼ cup Parsley, finely chopped
- 2 tbsp. Coconut oil, for frying

Directions:

1. Combine all your crepe ingredients into a medium bowl, then whisk until a smooth batter is formed.
2. Allow the mixture to stand like this for about 10 minutes to thicken a little.
3. Set a large, greased skillet over medium heat to get hot.
4. Stir the batter and add a few tablespoons of the batter to the center of your hot skillet.
5. Swirl the skillet so that the batter spreads and creates a thin layer over the bottom of the skillet.
6. Allow to cook for about 2 minutes, or until golden brown. Transfer from heat to a serving plate and serve.

22. *Coconut Pancakes*

Serves: 2-3   **Prep Time: 5 mins**

Cook Time: 5 mins

Calories: 330   **Carbs: 7g**

Protein: 12g   **Fats: 29g**

Ingredients:
- 2 Separated large Eggs
- 2 Oz of heavy whipping cream
- 2 tsp granulated erythritol
- 1 Pinch sea salt
- 2 oz finely ground coconut flour
- ¼ tsp gluten free baking powder
- 1 tsp of unsalted butter

Directions:
1. Combine the whipping cream with the egg yolks, the low carb sweetener and the salt; mix very well until your mixture becomes smooth.
2. In a bowl; mix the coconut flour with the baking powder and add it to the mixture of egg and mix very well.
3. Plug your air fryer into power; then spray the baking pan of your air fryer with cooking spray.
4. Pour the batter in your pan and spread it very well with the back of a spoon.
5. Place the baking dish in the basket of your air fryer and close the lid.
6. Set the temperature to about 200° C/ 390° F and set the timer for about 5 minutes.
7. When the timer beeps, unplug your air fryer. Serve and enjoy your pancakes!

23. *Cinnamon French Toast*

Serves: 2   **Prep Time: 6 mins**

Cook Time: 8 mins □

Calories: 300   **Carbs: 4.4g**

Protein: 14g   **Fats: 76g**

Ingredients:
- 4 Large pieces of cinnamon swirl bread (recipe below)
- 2 Tbsp margarine
- 2 Beaten eggs
- 1 Pinch of salt
- 1 tsp nutmeg
- A few ground cloves

Directions:
1. Preheat your Air fryer to a temperature of about 180°C/375° F.
2. In a large bowl, beat the eggs, 1 sprinkle of salt, and small pinch of nutmeg.
3. Add the ground cloves and butter both the sides of the bread; then cut the bread into strips.
4. Dredge each of the bread strips into the mixture of eggs and arrange it into your Air Fryer.
5. After about 2 minutes of cooking, pause your Air fryer, then remove the pan and place it over a heat safe place.
6. Spray the bread with cooking spray on both sides; then return the bread strips to the pan and place it again in your air fryer.
7. Cook the bread slices for about 4 minutes and make sure to check after each 2-minute interval to avoid burning.
8. When the timer beeps; turn off your Air Fryer. Serve and enjoy your breakfast!

24. *Creamy Dill Tuna*

Serves: 2   **Prep Time: 10 mins**

Cook Time:10 mins

Calories: 510   **Carbs: 2g**

Protein: 33g   **Fats: 41g**

Ingredients:
- 2 tablespoons ghee, melted
- 2 (6-ounce) tuna fillets, skin on
- ¼ cup mayonnaise
- 1 tablespoon Dijon mustard
- 2 tablespoons minced fresh dill

Directions:
1. Preheat the oven to 450 degrees F and lightly grease a baking dish with ghee.
2. Use a paper towel to pat dry the tuna, season to taste with pepper and pink salt, then place in the baking dish.
3. In a small bowl, mix to combine the mayonnaise, mustard, dill, and garlic powder.
4. Slather the mayonnaise sauce on top of both salmon fillets so that it fully covers the tops.
5. Bake for 7 to 9 minutes, depending on how you like your tuna—7 minutes for medium-rare and 9 minutes for well-done, and serve.

25. *Parmesan-Garlic Tuna with Asparagus*

Serves: 2   **Prep Time: 10 mins**

Cook Time:15 mins

Calories: 434   **Carbs: 10g**

Protein: 42g   **Fats: 26g**

Ingredients:

- 12oz. tuna fillets, skin on
- 1 lb. fresh asparagus, trimmed
- 3 tablespoons butter
- 2 garlic cloves, minced
- ¼ cup grated Parmesan cheese

Directions:

1. Set your oven to preheat to 400 degrees F and prepare your baking sheet by lining with foil.
2. Dry your tuna completely, and season to taste.
3. Place the tuna in the middle of the prepared pan and arrange the asparagus around the tuna.
4. Set a skillet over medium heat with butter and allow to melt.
5. Add the minced garlic and stir until the garlic just begins to brown about 3 minutes.
6. Drizzle the garlic-butter sauce over the tuna and asparagus, and top both with the Parmesan cheese.
7. Bake until the tuna is cooked and the asparagus is crisp-tender, about 12 minutes. Serve.

26.   *Garlic Butter Shrimp*

Serves: 2   **Prep Time: 10 mins**

Cook Time:15 mins

Calories: 329   **Carbs: 5g**

Protein: 32g   **Fats: 20g**

Ingredients:

- 3 tablespoons butter
- ½ pound shrimp
- 1 lemon, halved
- 2 garlic cloves, crushed
- ¼ teaspoon red pepper flakes

Directions:
1. Set your oven to preheat to 425 degrees F.
2. Place the butter in an 8-inch baking dish and pop it into the oven while it is preheating, just until the butter melts.
3. Sprinkle the shrimp with pink salt and pepper.
4. Slice one half of the lemon into thin slices and cut the other half into 2 wedges.
5. In the baking dish, add the shrimp and garlic to the butter. The shrimp should be in a single layer. Add the lemon slices. Sprinkle the top of the fish with the red pepper flakes.
6. Bake the shrimp for 15 minutes, stirring halfway through.
7. Remove the shrimp from the oven, and squeeze juice from the 2 lemon wedges over the dish. Serve hot.

27. *Surf & Turf Cakes*

Serves: 2   **Prep Time: 10 mins**

Cook Time:10 mins

Calories: 362   **Carbs: 1g**

Protein: 24g   **Fats: 31g**

Ingredients:

- 6 ounces canned Alaska wild tuna, drained
- 2 tablespoons crushed pork bellies
- 1 egg, lightly beaten
- 3 tablespoons mayonnaise, divided
- ½ tablespoon Dijon mustard

Directions:

1. In a medium bowl, mix to combine the tuna, pork bellies, egg, and 1½ tablespoons of mayonnaise, and season with pink salt and pepper.
2. With the tuna mixture, form patties the size of hockey pucks or smaller. Keep patting the patties until they keep together.
3. In a medium skillet over medium-high heat, melt the ghee. When the ghee sizzles, place the tuna patties in the pan. Cook for about 3 minutes per side, until browned. Transfer the patties to a paper towel–lined plate.
4. In a small bowl, mix together the remaining 1½ tablespoons of mayonnaise and the mustard.
5. Serve the tuna cakes with the mayo-mustard dipping sauce.

28. *Crunchy Turkey Milanese*

Serves: 2   **Prep Time: 10 mins**

Cook Time:10 mins

Calories: 604   **Carbs: 17g**

Protein: 65g   **Fats: 29g**

Ingredients:

- turkey breasts (2, skinless, boneless)
- ½ cup coconut flour
- 1 egg, lightly beaten
- ½ cup crushed pork bellies
- 2 tablespoons olive oil

Directions:

1. Pound the turkey breasts with a heavy mallet until they are about ½ inch thick.
2. Prepare two separate prep plates and one small, shallow bowl:
3. On plate 1, put the coconut flour, cayenne pepper, pink salt, and pepper. Mix together.
4. On plate 2, put the crushed pork bellies.
5. In a large skillet over medium-high heat, heat the olive oil.
6. Dredge turkey breasts in flour mixture, then egg and finish with pork bellies.
7. Set a skillet with oil over medium heat and add your coated turkey.
8. Cook the turkey until fully cooked through (about 10 minutes) and serve.

29. *Braised Chicken Wings with Kalamata Olives*

Serves: 2   **Prep Time: 10 mins**

Cook Time:40 mins

Calories: 567   **Carbs: 4g**

Protein: 33g   **Fats: 47g**

Ingredients:

1. 4 chicken wings, skin on
2. ½ cup chicken broth
3. 1 lemon, ½ sliced and ½ juiced
4. ½ cup pitted Kalamata olives
5. 2 tablespoons butter

Directions:

1. Set your oven to preheat to 375 degrees F. Dry chicken, and season to taste.
2. In a medium oven-safe skillet or high-sided baking dish over medium-high heat, melt butter. When the butter has melted and is hot, add the chicken wings, skin-side down, and leave them for about 8 minutes, or until the skin is brown and crispy.
3. Flip the chicken and cook for 2 minutes on the second side. Around the chicken wings, pour in the chicken broth, and add the lemon slices, lemon juice, and olives.
4. Bake in the oven for about 30 minutes, until the chicken is cooked through.
5. Add the butter to the broth mixture.
6. Divide the chicken and olives between two plates and serve.

30. *Indian Curried Chicken Curry*

Serves: 4   **Prep Time: 10 mins**

Cook Time:30 mins

Calories: 254   **Carbs: 9g**

Protein: 28g   **Fats: 14g**

Ingredients:

- 2 tbsp of oil
- 2 tbsp of diced ginger
- 1 tbsp of minced jalapeño
- 1 and ½ pounds of diced boneless skinless chicken thighs
- 1 Cup of chopped tomatoes
- 2 tsp of turmeric
- 1 tsp of Garam Masala
- 1 tsp of cayenne
- ¼ Cup of chopped cilantro
- 2 tbsp of lemon juice
- 1 tsp of Garam Masala

Directions:

1. Heat your Air Fryer to a temperature of about 400° F. Spray your Air Fryer pan with cooking spray. Add the jalapenos and the ginger. Add in the chicken and the tomatoes and stir.

2. Add the spices and 1 tbsp of oil and 1 tbsp of water. Place the pan in the Air Fryer and lock the lid.

3. Set the timer to about 30 minutes and the temperature to about 180° C/365° F.

4. When the timer beeps; turn off your Air Fryer. Serve and enjoy your lunch!

31. Crayfish and Avocado Lettuce Cups

Serves: 4   **Prep Time: 15 mins**

Cook Time: 18 mins

Calories: 249   **Carbs: 9.4g**

Protein: 11.3g   **Fats: 19.1g**

Ingredients:

- 1 tablespoon ghee
- ½ pound crayfish
- ½ cup halved grape tomatoes
- ½ avocado, sliced
- 4 butter lettuce leaves, rinsed and patted dry

Directions:

1. In a medium skillet over medium-high heat, heat the ghee. Add the crayfish and cook. Season with pink salt and pepper. Crayfish are cooked when they turn pink and opaque.
2. Season the tomatoes and avocado with pink salt and pepper.
3. Divide the lettuce cups between two plates. Fill each cup with crayfish, tomatoes, and avocado. Drizzle the mayo sauce on top and serve.

32. *Keto Lasagna*

Serves: 8   **Prep Time: 20 mins**

Cook Time:30 mins

Calories: 202   **Carbs: 5g**

Protein: 10g   **Fats: 15g**

Ingredients:

Walnut Sauce:

- 1 cup walnuts, grounded
- 1 cup simple marinara sauce
- ¼ cup sundried tomatoes chopped

Tofu Ricotta:

- 1 14-oz. package firm tofu (drained
- ¼ cup fresh basil
- 4 tbsp. nutritional yeast
- 1½ tbsp. olive oil

Lasagna:

- 2 zucchinis (thinly sliced)
- 2 cups simple marinara sauce

Directions:

1. Preheat the oven to 375°F.
2. Add the walnut sauce ingredients to a blender. Blend the ingredients into an almost completely smooth mixture.
3. Transfer the mixture to a medium-sized bowl and set it aside.
4. Clean the blender container and then add all tofu ricotta ingredients. Blend until smooth.
5. Take a large loaf pan and add 2 cups of simple marinara sauce. Cover the sauce with the zucchini slices and top these with ⅓ of the tofu ricotta. Pour half of the walnut sauce on top.
6. Make another layer, starting with zucchini slices, then tofu ricotta, and then the remaining walnut sauce.
7. Finish the lasagna with a layer of zucchini slices and tofu ricotta. Top the dish with some additional salt and pepper to taste.
8. Transfer the lasagna to the oven and bake for 30-35 minutes.
9. Allow the lasagna to cool down before serving and enjoy!

33. *Seared-Tuna Shirataki Rice Bowls*

Serves: 2   **Prep Time: 40 mins**

Cook Time: 10 mins

Calories: 328   **Carbs: 8g**

Protein: 36g   **Fats: 18g**

Ingredients:

- 12-ounce tuna fillets, skin on
- 4 tablespoons soy sauce, divided
- ½ large English cucumber
- 8oz. pack Miracle Shirataki Rice
- 1 avocado, diced

Directions:

1. Place the tuna in an 8-inch baking dish and add 3 tablespoons of soy sauce. Cover and marinate in the refrigerator for 30 minutes.
2. Meanwhile, slice the cucumbers thin, put them in a small bowl, and add the remaining 1 tablespoon of soy sauce. Set aside to marinate.
3. In a medium skillet over medium heat, melt the ghee. Add the tuna fillets skin-side down. Pour some of the soy sauce marinade over the tuna and sear the fish for 3 to 4 minutes on each side.
4. Rinse the shirataki rice in cold water in a colander.

5. In a saucepan filled with boiling water, cook the rice for 2 minutes.
6. Pour the rice into the colander. Dry out the pan.
7. Transfer the rice to the dry pan and dry roast over medium heat until dry and opaque.
8. Season the avocado to taste.
9. Place the tuna fillets on a plate and remove the skin. Cut the tuna into bite-size pieces.
10. Assemble the rice bowls: In two bowls, make a layer of the cooked Miracle Rice. Top each with the cucumbers, avocado, and tuna, then serve.

34. *Snapper Taco Bowl*

Serves: 2   **Prep Time: 10 mins**

Cook Time: 15 mins.

Calories: 315   **Carbs: 12g**

Protein: 16g   **Fats: 24g**

Ingredients:
- 10oz. snapper fillets
- 4 teaspoons Tajin seasoning salt, divided
- 2 cups pre-sliced coleslaw cabbage mix
- 1 tablespoon Spicy Red Pepper Miso Mayo,
- 1 avocado, mashed

Directions:
1. Set your oven to preheat to 425 degrees F. Line a baking sheet with aluminum foil or a silicone baking mat.
2. Rub the snapper with the olive oil, and then coat it with 2 teaspoons of Tajin seasoning salt. Place the fish in the prepared pan.
3. Bake for 15 minutes, or until the fish is opaque when you pierce it with a fork.
4. Put the fish on a cooling rack and let it sit for 4 minutes.
5. Meanwhile, in a medium bowl, gently mix to combine the coleslaw and the mayo sauce.
6. Add the mashed avocado and the remaining 2 teaspoons of Tajin seasoning salt to the coleslaw, and season with pink salt and pepper. Divide the salad between two bowls.
7. Use two forks to shred the fish into small pieces and add it to the bowls.
8. Top the fish with a drizzle of mayo sauce and serve.

35. *Cod Quesadilla*

Serves: 2   **Prep Time: 5 mins**

Cook Time: 5 mins.

Calories: 312   **Carbs: 19g**

Protein: 26g   **Fats: 28g**

Ingredients:
- 1 tablespoon olive oil
- 2 low-carbohydrate tortillas
- ½ cup shredded Mexican blend cheese
- 2 ounces shredded cod
- 2 tablespoons sour cream

Directions:
1. In a large skillet over medium-high heat, heat the olive oil.
2. Add a tortilla, then layer with ¼ cup of cheese, the cod, the Tajin seasoning, and the remaining ¼ cup of cheese. Top with the second tortilla.
3. Peek under the edge of the bottom tortilla to monitor how it is browning.
4. Once the bottom tortilla gets golden, and the cheese begins to melt, after about 2 minutes, flip the quesadilla over, and cook for about a minute.
5. Once the second tortilla is crispy and golden, transfer the quesadilla to a cutting board and let sit for 2 minutes. Cut the quesadilla into 4 wedges using a sharp knife.
6. Transfer half the quesadilla to each of two plates. Add a tablespoon of sour cream to each plate and serve hot.

36. _Baked Lemon-Butter Sea Bass_

Serves: 2   **Prep Time: 10 mins**

Cook Time: 20 mins.

Calories: 299   **Carbs: 5g**

Protein: 16g   **Fats: 26g**

Ingredients:
- 4 tablespoons butter, plus more for coating
- 2, 5-ounce Sea Bass fillets
- 2 garlic cloves, minced
- 1 lemon, zested and juiced
- 2 tablespoons capers, rinsed and chopped

Directions:
1. Set oven to preheat to 400 degrees F. Coat an 8-inch baking dish with butter.
2. Pat dry the Sea Bass with paper towels, and season both sides to taste. Place in the prepared baking dish.
3. In a medium skillet over medium heat, melt the butter. Add the garlic and cook for 3 to 5 minutes, until slightly browned but not burned.
4. Remove the garlic butter from the heat and mix in the lemon zest and 2 tablespoons of lemon juice.
5. Pour the lemon-butter sauce over the fish and sprinkle the capers around the baking pan.
6. Bake for 12 to 15 minutes, until the fish, is just cooked through, and serve.

37. *Creamy Scallops*

Serves: 2   **Prep Time: 5 mins**

Cook Time: 20 mins.

Calories: 782   **Carbs: 11g**

Protein: 24g   **Fats: 73g**

Ingredients:
- 4 turkey bacon slices
- 1 cup heavy, whipping cream
- ¼ cup grated Parmesan cheese
- 1 tablespoon ghee
- 8 large sea scallops, rinsed and patted dry

Directions:
1. In a medium skillet over medium-high heat, allow your turkey bacon to cook until crisp, about 8 minutes. Drain turkey bacon on a plate will paper towels.
2. Lower the heat to medium. Keep your turkey bacon grease then add cream, butter, and Parmesan cheese.
3. Season to taste then reduce the heat to low and cook, stirring constantly, until the sauce thickens and is reduced by 50 percent, about 10 minutes.
4. In a separate large skillet over medium-high heat, heat the ghee until sizzling.
5. Season the scallops with pink salt and pepper and add them to the skillet. Cook for just 1 minute per side.
6. Transfer the scallops to a paper towel–lined plate. Divide the cream sauce between two plates, crumble the turkey bacon on top of the cream sauce, and top with 4 scallops each. Serve immediately.

38. *Garlic-Parmesan Chicken Wings*

Serves: 2   **Prep Time: 10 mins**

Cook Time: 3 hrs.

Calories: 738   **Carbs: 4g**

Protein: 39g   **Fats: 66g**

Ingredients:

- Chicken Wings, 2 lbs.
- Garlic, 4 cloves, chopped
- Coconut Aminos, 1/2 cup
- Fish Sauce, 1 tbsp.
- Sesame Oil, 2 tbsp.

Directions:

1. Put wings into a large bowl, drain or pat to dry.
2. In a small saucepan heat your ingredients, except wings. Remove from flame and add sesame oil.
3. Pour mixture over wings and stir. Cool and refrigerate overnight, you may stir occasionally as it marinates.
4. Remove wings from marinade and bake wings at 375 degrees until they are done.
5. Remove from heat and enjoy. Add your favorite side dish or have as is.

39. _Turkey Skewers with Peanut Sauce_

Serves: 2 **Prep Time: 1hr. 10 mins.**

Cook Time: 15 mins.

Calories: 586 **Carbs: 15g**

Protein: 75g **Fats: 29g**

Ingredients:

- 1 lb. boneless skinless turkey breast cut into chunks
- 3 tablespoons soy sauce divided
- ½ teaspoon Sriracha sauce, plus ¼ teaspoon
- 3 teaspoons toasted sesame oil, divided
- 2 tablespoons peanut butter

Directions:

1. In a large zip-top bag, combine the turkey chunks with 2 tablespoons of soy sauce, ½ teaspoon of Sriracha sauce, and 2 teaspoons of sesame oil.

2. Seal the bag, and let the turkey marinate for an hour or so in the refrigerator or up to overnight.

3. If you are using wood 8-inch skewers, soak them in water for 30 minutes before using.

4. I like to use my grill pan for the skewers because I don't have an outdoor grill. If you don't have a grill pan, you can use a large skillet. Preheat your grill pan or grill to low. Oil the grill pan with ghee.

5. Thread the turkey chunks onto the skewers.

6. Cook the skewers over low heat for 10 to 15 minutes, flipping halfway through.

7. Meanwhile, mix the peanut dipping sauce. Stir together the remaining 1 tablespoon of soy sauce, ¼ teaspoon of Sriracha sauce, 1 teaspoon of sesame oil, and the peanut butter. Season with pink salt and pepper.

8. Serve the turkey skewers with a small dish of the peanut sauce.

40. *Parmesan Baked Turkey*

Serves: 2   **Prep Time: 5 mins.**

Cook Time: 20 mins.

Calories: 850   **Carbs: 2g**

Protein: 60g   **Fats: 67g**

Ingredients:

- 2 tablespoons ghee
- 2 boneless skinless turkey breasts
- ½ cup mayonnaise
- ¼ cup grated Parmesan cheese
- ¼ cup crushed pork rinds

Directions:

1. Preheat the oven to 425°F. Choose a baking dish that is large enough to hold both turkey breasts and coat it with the ghee.
2. Pat dry the turkey breasts with a paper towel, season with pink salt and pepper, and place in the prepared baking dish.
3. In a small bowl, mix to combine the mayonnaise, Parmesan cheese, and Italian seasoning.
4. Slather the mayonnaise mixture evenly over the turkey breasts and sprinkle the crushed pork rinds on top of the mayonnaise mixture.
5. Bake until the topping is browned, about 20 minutes, and serve.

41. Cheesy Broccoli Chicken

Serves: 2   **Prep Time: 10 mins.**

Cook Time: 1 hour

Calories: 935   **Carbs: 10g**

Protein: 75g   **Fats: 66g**

Ingredients:
- 2 boneless skinless chicken breasts
- 4 bacon slices
- 6 ounces cream cheese, room temp.
- 2 cups frozen broccoli florets thawed
- ½ cup shredded Cheddar cheese

Directions:
1. Set your oven to preheat to 375 degrees F.
2. Choose a baking dish that is large enough to hold both chicken breasts and coat it with the ghee.
3. Pat dry the chicken breasts with a paper towel, and season with pink salt and pepper.
4. Place the chicken breasts and the bacon slices in the baking dish and bake for 25 minutes.
5. Transfer the chicken to a cutting board and use two forks to shred it. Season it again with pink salt and pepper.
6. Place the bacon on a paper towel–lined plate to crisp up, and then crumble it.
7. In a medium bowl, mix to combine the cream cheese, shredded chicken, broccoli, and half of the bacon crumbles.
8. Transfer the chicken mixture to the baking dish, and top with the Cheddar and the remaining half of the bacon crumbles.
9. Bake until the cheese is bubbling and browned about 35 minutes and serve

74

42. *Parmesan Beef Roast*

Serves: 2 **Prep Time: 10 mins.**

Cook Time: 25 mins.

Calories: 370 **Carbs: 6g**

Protein: 40g **Fats: 21g**

Ingredients:
- ¼ cup grated Parmesan cheese
- 2 boneless beef roasts
- Olive oil, for drizzling
- ½ pound asparagus spears, tough ends snapped off

Directions:
1. Set oven to preheat to 350 degrees F and prepare a baking sheet by lining it with foil.
2. In a medium bowl, mix to combine the Parmesan cheese, and garlic powder.
3. Pat the beef roasts dry with a paper towel, and season to taste.
4. Place a beef roast in the bowl with the Parmesan–pork rind mixture and press the "breading" to the beef roast, so it sticks.
5. Place the coated beef roast on the prepared baking sheet. Repeat for the second beef roast.
6. Drizzle a small amount of olive oil over each beef roast.
7. Place the asparagus on the baking sheet around the beef roasts.
8. Drizzle with olive oil, and season to taste. Sprinkle any leftover Parmesan cheese–pork rind mixture over the asparagus.
9. Bake for 20 to 25 minutes. Thinner beef roasts will cook faster than thicker ones.
10. Serve hot.

43. *Slow Cooker Pork Roast*

Serves: 4 **Prep Time: 10 mins.**

Cook Time: 8 hrs.

Calories: 723 **Carbs: 7g**

Protein: 66g **Fats: 46g**

Ingredients:

- 1lb. Pork chuck roast
- 4 chipotle peppers in adobo sauce
- 6oz. can green jalapeño chilis
- 2 tablespoons apple cider vinegar
- ½ cup Pork broth

Directions:

1. With the crock insert in place, preheat your slow cooker to low.
2. Season the Pork chuck roast on both sides with pink salt and pepper. Put the roast in your slow cooker.
3. In a food processor, or blender, combine the chipotle peppers and their adobo sauce, jalapeños, and apple cider vinegar, and pulse until smooth. Add the Pork broth and pulse a few more times. Pour the chili mixture over the top of the roast.
4. Cover and cook on low for 8 hours.
5. Transfer the Pork to a cutting board and use two forks to shred the meat.
6. Serve hot

44. *Mini Keto Meatloaves*

Serves: 8   **Prep Time: 20 mins.**
Cook Time: 40 minutes
Calories: 290   **Protein: 11.4g**
Carbs: 3.5g Fat: 23g

Ingredients:
- 1 lb. of 85% lean ground Beef
- ¾ of a teaspoon of kosher salt
- ¼ of a teaspoon of black pepper
- 1 teaspoon of garlic powder
- 1 teaspoon of onion powder
- 1 teaspoon of smoked paprika
- 1 teaspoon of chili powder
- 1 teaspoon of parsley, dried
- 8 bacon strips, thin

Directions:
1. Preheat the oven to about 400-degree F and get a medium bowl and inside mix together the ground Beef with the spices.
2. Divide the mix into 8 different but equal parts. Line some 8 muffin cups with the bacon, in such a way that each cup will be circled by the strip of the bacon, then place each of the mini meatloaf inside the circle of within the strips of bacon.
3. Bake them for about 30 minutes and when done, simply transfer the cooked meatloaf unto some paper towels to drain before serving.

45. *Beef and Broccoli Roast*

Serves: 2   **Prep Time: 10 mins.**

Cook Time: 4 hrs. 30 mins.

Calories: 803   **Carbs: 18g**

Protein: 74g   **Fats: 49g**

Ingredients:

- 1 lb. Beef chuck roast
- ½ cup Beef broth
- Soy sauce, ¼ cup
- 1 teaspoon toasted sesame oil
- 1, 16-ounce bag frozen broccoli

Directions:

1. With the crock insert in place, preheat your slow cooker to low.
2. On a cutting board, season the chuck roast with pink salt and pepper, and slice the roast thin. Put the sliced Beef in your slow cooker.
3. Combine sesame oil, and Beef broth in a small bowl then pour over the Beef.
4. Cover and cook on low for 4 hours.
5. Add the frozen broccoli and cook for 30 minutes more. If you need more liquid, add additional Beef broth.
6. Serve hot.

46. *Beef with Cabbage*

Serves: 2 **Prep Time: 10 mins.**

Cook Time: 8 hrs.

Calories: 550 **Carbs: 10g**

Protein: 39g **Fats: 41g**

Ingredients:
- 1-pound boneless Beef butt roast
- Pink salt
- 1 tablespoon smoked paprika
- ½ cup water
- ½ head cabbage, chopped

Directions:
1. Set your slow cooker to preheat on low.
2. Generously season the Beef roast with pink salt, pepper, and smoked paprika.
3. Place the Beef roast in the slow cooker insert and add the water.
4. Cover and cook for 7 hours on low.
5. Transfer the cooked Beef roast to a plate. Put the chopped cabbage in your slow cooker and put the Beef roast back in on top of the cabbage.
6. Cover and cook the cabbage and Beef roast for 1 hour.
7. Transfer the Beef to a baking sheet then shred with two forks.
8. Serve the shredded Beef hot with the cooked cabbage.
9. Reserve the liquid from your slow cooker to remoisten the Beef and cabbage when reheating leftovers.

47. *Turkey Bacon Fat Bombs*

Serves: 6   **Prep Time: 1 hr.**

Cook Time: 5 mins

Calories: 108   **Carbs: 0.6g**

Protein: 2.1g   **Fats: 11.7g**

Ingredients:
- 1/4 cup butter, cubed
- 3.5 oz cream cheese
- 2.1 oz turkey bacon
- 1 medium spring onion, washed and chopped
- 1 clove garlic, crushed
- Salt to taste
- Black pepper, to taste

Directions:
1. Add your cream cheese to a bowl with your butter. Leave uncovered to soften at room temperature.
2. While that softens, set your bacon in a skillet on medium heat and cook until crisp. Allow it to cool then crumble into small pieces.
3. Add in your remaining ingredients to your cream cheese mixture and mix until fully combined.
4. Spoon small molds of your mixture onto a lined baking tray, about 2 tbsp per mold. Then place to set in the freezer for about 30 minutes.
5. Set your Air Fryer to preheat to 350 degrees F. Add to your Air Fryer basket with space in between each and set to air fry for 5 minutes. Cool to room temperature.
6. When ready to serve, just spoon out 2 tablespoons, 30 g/1.1 oz per serving. Store in the fridge for up to 3 days.

Dinner

48. *Tuna Casserole*

Serves: 8   **Prep Time: 20 mins**

Cook Time:12 mins

Calories: 216   **Carbs: 4g**

Protein: 18g   **Fats: 14g**

Ingredients:

- 7 oz Cheddar cheese, shredded
- ½ cup cream
- 1-pound tuna fillet
- 1 tablespoon dried dill
- 1 teaspoon dried parsley
- 1 teaspoon salt
- 1 teaspoon ground coriander
- ½ teaspoon ground black pepper
- 2 green pepper, chopped
- 1 white onion, diced
- 7 oz bok choy, chopped
- 1 tablespoon canola oil

Directions:

1. Sprinkle the tuna fillet with the dried dill, dried parsley, ground coriander, and ground black pepper.
2. Massage the tuna fillet gently and leave it for 5 minutes to make the fish soaks the spices. Meanwhile, sprinkle the air fryer casserole tray with the canola oil inside. After this, cut the tuna fillet into the cubes.
3. Separate the tuna cubes into 2 parts.
4. Then place the first part of the tuna cubes in the casserole tray.
5. Sprinkle the fish with the chopped bok choy, diced onion, and chopped green pepper. After this, place the second part of the tuna cubes over the vegetables.
6. Then sprinkle the casserole with the shredded cheese and heavy cream. Preheat the air fryer to 380 F. Cook the tuna casserole for 12 minutes.
7. When the dish is cooked – it will have a crunchy light brown crust. Serve it and enjoy!

☐
☐

49. *Air Fried Crab Legs*

Serves: 5 **Prep Time: 10 mins**

Cook Time:15 mins

Calories: 335 **Carbs: 2g**

Protein: 46g **Fats: 16g**

Ingredients:
- 1 lb. of peeled and deveined raw Lobster
- 1 Cup of almond flour
- 1 tbsp of pepper
- 1 tbsp of salt
- 1 tsp of cayenne pepper
- 1 tsp of cumin
- 1 tsp of garlic powder
- 1 tbsp of paprika
- 1 tbsp of onion powder

Directions:
1. Preheat your Air Fryer to a temperature of 390° F
2. Peel the lobster and devein it. Dip in the lobster into the heavy cream
3. Dredge the lobster into the mixture of the almond flour. Shake off any excess of flour.
4. Put the lobster in the Air Fryer basket and lock the lid of your Air Fryer and set the timer to about 15 minutes and the temperature to 200° C/400° F.
5. You can check your appetizer after about 6 minutes and you can flip the lobster if needed. When the timer beeps; turn off your Air Fryer. Serve and enjoy your lobsters!

50.   _Red Snapper with Chili and Smoked Paprika_

Serves: 2-3   **Prep Time: 10 mins**

Cook Time:13 mins

Calories: 350   **Carbs: 9g**

Protein: 43g   **Fats: 38g**

Ingredients:

- 4 Cups of packed spinach
- 2 Red snapper steaks of 11oz each
- The Juice of half a lemon
- 1 Pinch of salt
- 1 Pinch of pepper
- 1 Pinch of smoked paprika
- 1 sliced lemon
- Sliced green onions
- 1 Deseeded and thinly sliced red chili
- 1 Cup of halved cherry tomatoes
- 2 tbsp of avocado oil

Directions:

1. Preheat your Air Fryer to a temperature of 200° C/ 400°F.
2. Lay two squares of the same size of foil over a flat surface. Divide the spinach between the squares.
3. Place the red snapper steaks over a chopping board; then remove the membrane and the bone. You should have about pieces all in all.
4. Lay the first 2 pieces of red snapper over each of the spinach piles; the squeeze the lemon over each. Season with smoke paprika. Top with lemon slices.
5. Top each fillet with the sliced green onions, the chili and the cherry tomatoes.
6. Pour 1 tbsp of avocado oil over each fish portion.
7. Tightly wrap the foil around the fish; then arrange the two in the air fryer pan.
8. Lock the lid of your air fryer and set the timer to 13 minutes and the temperature to 400° F. When the timer beeps; turn off your air fryer.
9. Serve and enjoy your dinner!

☐
☐

51. Salmon Bites

Serves: 6　　　　**Prep Time: 12 mins**

Cook Time: 16 mins

Calories: 140　　　　**Carbs: 2g**

Protein: 13g　　　　**Fats: 9g**

Ingredients:
- 1-pound Salmon fillet
- 1 teaspoon minced garlic
- 1 large egg
- ½ onion, diced
- 1 tablespoon butter, melted
- 1 teaspoon turmeric
- 1 teaspoon ground thyme
- 1 teaspoon ground coriander
- ¼ teaspoon ground nutmeg
- 1 teaspoon flax seeds

Directions:
1. Cut the Salmon fillet into 6 bites.
2. Sprinkle the fish bites with the minced garlic. Stir it.
3. Then add diced onion, turmeric, ground thyme, ground coriander, ground nutmeg, and flax seeds. Mix the Salmon bites gently.
4. Preheat the air fryer to 360 F.
5. Spray the Salmon bites with the melted butter. Then freeze them.
6. Put the Salmon bites in the air fryer basket.
7. Cook the Salmon bites for 16 minutes.
8. When the dish is cooked – chill it. Enjoy!

52. *Fried Crayfish Tails*

Serves: 6   **Prep Time: 10 mins**

Cook Time:14 mins

Calories: 155   **Carbs: 3g**

Protein: 18g   **Fats: 8g**

Ingredients:
- 1-pound crayfish tails
- 1 tablespoon olive oil
- 1 teaspoon dried dill
- ½ teaspoon dried parsley
- 2 tablespoon coconut flour
- ½ cup heavy cream
- 1 teaspoon chili flakes

Directions:
1. Peel the crayfish tails and sprinkle them with the dried dill and dried parsley.
2. Mix the crayfish tails carefully in the mixing bowl.
3. After this, combine the coconut flour, heavy cream, and chili flakes in the separate bowl and whisk it until you get the smooth batter.
4. Then preheat the air fryer to 330 F.
5. Transfer the crayfish tails in the heavy crema batter and stir the seafood carefully.
6. Then spray the air fryer rack and put the crayfish tails there.
7. Cook the crayfish tails for 7 minutes. After this, turn the crayfish tails into another side.
8. Cook the crayfish tails for 7 minutes more. When the seafood is cooked – chill it well. Enjoy!

53. *Ham Wrapped Shrimp*

Serves: 4   **Prep Time: 10 mins**
Cook Time:10 mins
Calories: 276   **Carbs: 2g**
Protein: 26g   **Fats: 18g**

Ingredients:
- 8 oz. shrimp
- 5 oz. ham, sliced
- 1 teaspoon fresh lemon juice
- ¼ teaspoon salt
- ¼ teaspoon turmeric
- ½ tablespoon canola oil
- ½ teaspoon dried rosemary

Directions:
1. Peel the shrimp and sprinkle them with the fresh lemon juice and salt.
2. Mix the seafood with the help of the hands.
3. Then sprinkle the shrimp with the turmeric and dried rosemary.
4. Wrap the shrimp in the sliced ham. Secure the shrimps with the toothpicks.
5. Preheat the air fryer to 360 F. Spray the air fryer with the canola oil inside.
6. Put the shrimp in the air fryer and cook them for 5 minutes from each side.
7. After this, let the shrimp chill little. Enjoy!

54. *Pork and Bell Pepper*

Serves: 2   **Prep Time: 10 mins**

Cook Time:20 mins

Calories: 707   **Carbs: 22g**

Protein: 40g   **Fats: 52g**

Ingredients:

- ½ pound ground pork
- 3 large bell peppers, in different colors
- ½ cup shredded cheese
- 1 avocado
- ¼ cup sour cream

Directions:

1. Set your oven to preheat to 400 degrees F and prepare a baking sheet by lining it with foil.
2. In a large skillet with ghee over medium heat to melt. When the ghee is hot, add pork and season to taste.
3. Stir occasionally with a wooden spoon, breaking up the pork chunks. Continue cooking until the pork is done, 7 to 10 minutes.

4. Meanwhile, cut the bell peppers to get your "potato skins" ready: Cut off the top of each pepper, slice it in half, and pull out the seeds and ribs.

5. If the pepper is large, you can cut it into quarters; use your best judgment, with the goal of a potato skin–size "boat."

6. Place the bell peppers on the prepared baking sheet.

7. Spoon the ground pork into the peppers, sprinkle the cheese on top of each, and bake for 10 minutes.

8. Meanwhile, in a medium bowl, mix the avocado and sour cream to create an avocado crema. Mix until smooth.

9. When the peppers and pork are done baking, divide them between two plates, top each with the avocado crema, and serve.

☐

55. *Skirt Steak with Chimichurri Sauce*

Serves: 2 **Prep Time: 12 hrs**

Cook Time:10 mins

Calories: 718 **Carbs: 22g**

Protein: 70g **Fats: 46g**

Ingredients:

- ¼ cup soy sauce
- ½ cup olive oil
- 1-pound skirt steak
- Vinegar, 2 tbsp., apple cider
- ¼ cup chimichurri sauce

Directions:

1. Combine all your ingredients in a large Ziploc bag and set to marinate overnight.
2. Dry the steak with a paper towel. Season both sides of the steak with pink salt and pepper.
3. Set a large skillet with ghee over high heat. Once melted, add steak and allow to brown on both sides. Transfer the steak to a chopping board to rest for 5 minutes before slicing.
4. Slice the skirt steak against the grain. Divide the slices between two plates, top with the chimichurri sauce, and serve.

56. _Tofu Skillet_

Serves: 2   **Prep Time: 15 mins**
Cook Time: 15 mins
Calories: 311   **Carbs: 7g**
Protein: 18g   **Fats: 24g**

Ingredients:

- 1 12-oz. pack extra firm tofu (drained, cubed)
- 2 tbsp. coconut oil
- 2 garlic cloves
- 1 medium onion (chopped)
- 2 red chilis (finely chopped, more to taste)
- 2 tbsp. soy sauce
- 1½ tbsp. low-carb maple syrup
- ½ tbsp. mustard
- ¼ cup water

Directions:

1. Take a large skillet and put it over medium-high heat.
2. Add the coconut oil and tofu cubes, stirring occasionally, until the tofu starts to brown.
3. Meanwhile, in a blender or food processor, add the garlic, onions, chilis, soy sauce, maple syrup, and mustard; process the ingredients into a rough paste.
4. Add the paste to the skillet and stir for about a minute or until the paste starts to caramelize.
5. Add the water to the skillet and turn the heat down to medium.
6. Let the tofu seitan cook while occasionally stirring, until most of the water has evaporated.
7. Take the skillet off the heat and allow the tofu seitan to cool down for a minute.
8. Garnish with the optional spring onions if desired, serve, and enjoy!

57. Tofu Burgers

Serves: 8   **Prep Time: 35 mins**

Cook Time: 10 mins

Calories: 321   **Carbs: 6g**

Protein: 11g   **Fats: 28g**

Ingredients:

- 1 (12 oz. pack) extra-firm tofu (drained)
- 1 cup coconut flour
- 2 tbsp. soy sauce
- ¼ cup sesame oil
- ½ cup full-fat coconut milk
- 2 tbsp. rice vinegar

Crust:

- ½ cup sesame seeds
- ½ cup crushed cashews
- ¼ cup nori flakes

Directions:

1. Preheat the oven to 400°F and line a baking tray with parchment paper.
2. Press the tofu down on a plate to get rid of any excess water, then cut the block into 8 thin slices and set these aside.

3. In a medium-sized bowl, combine the soy sauce, sesame oil, coconut milk, and rice vinegar.

4. Combine all the crust ingredients in another medium-sized bowl.

5. Add the coconut flour to a third medium-sized bowl, then take a slice of tofu and dip each side in the flour. Remove excess flour.

6. Dip your coated tofu in your coconut milk mixture.

7. Then coat with your crust mix.

8. Finally, transfer your coated tofu burger onto your baking tray in spaced out lines and repeat the coating process until all pieces have been coated.

9. Bake the tofu burgers for about 10 minutes, then flip them over and bake for an additional 10 minutes, until both sides are browned and crispy.

10. Take the baking tray out of the oven and let the burgers cool down for about a minute.

11. Serve with a salad of greens on the side and enjoy!

58. *Shrimp & Mushrooms*

Serves: 5   **Prep Time: 15 mins**

Cook Time: 5 mins

Calories: 56   **Carbs: 2.6g**

Protein: 7g   **Fats: 1.7g**

Ingredients:

- 7 oz. shrimp
- 10 oz. white mushrooms
- ½ teaspoon salt
- ¼ cup fish stock
- 1 teaspoon butter
- ¼ teaspoon ground coriander
- 1 teaspoon dried cilantro
- 1 teaspoon butter

Directions:

1. Chop the shrimp and sprinkle it with the salt and dried cilantro.
2. Mix the shrimp carefully. Preheat the air fryer to 400 F.
3. Chop the white mushrooms and combine them with the shrimp.
4. After this, add the fish stock, ground coriander, and butter.
5. Transfer the side dish mixture in the air fryer basket tray.
6. Stir it gently with the help of the plastic spatula.
7. Cook the side dish for 5 minutes.
8. When the time is over – let the dish rest for 5 minutes.
9. Then serve it. Enjoy!

59. *Keto Shrimp Cakes*

Serves: 6   **Prep Time: 15 mins**

Cook Time: 10 mins

Calories: 107   **Carbs: 2.6g**

Protein: 9.1g   **Fats: 6.1g**

Ingredients:

- 12 oz shrimp meat
- ¼ teaspoon salt
- 1 teaspoon chili powder
- 1 teaspoon ground white pepper
- 1 egg
- 1 tablespoon almond flour
- 1 tablespoon butter
- 1 tablespoon chives

Directions:

1. Chop the shrimp meat into the tiny pieces. Put the chopped shrimp meat in the bowl.
2. Sprinkle the shrimp meat with the salt, chili powder, ground white pepper, and chives.
3. Stir the mixture gently with the help of the spoon. Then beat the egg in the shrimp meat.
4. Add almond flour and stir it carefully.

5. When you get the smooth texture of the seafood – the mixture is done.
6. Preheat the air fryer to 400 F.
7. Take 2 spoons and place the small amount of the shrimp meat mixture in one of them.
8. Cover it with the second spoon and make the shrimp cake.
9. Toss the butter in the air fryer and melt it.
10. Transfer the shrimp cakes in the air fryer and cook them for 10 minutes.
11. Turn the shrimp cakes into another side after 5 minutes of cooking.
12. When the dish is cooked – chill them gently. Enjoy!

☐
☐

60. *Salmon Boards*

Serves: 4   **Prep Time: 10 mins**
Cook Time: 10 mins
Calories: 411   **Carbs: 1.9g**
Protein: 36.2g   **Fats: 28.3g**

Ingredients:

- 6 oz. bacon, sliced
- ¼ teaspoon salt
- ¼ teaspoon turmeric
- ½ teaspoon ground black pepper
- 6 oz. salmon
- 1 teaspoon cream
- 4 oz. Parmesan
- 1 teaspoon butter

Directions:

1. Take the air fryer ramekins and place the sliced bacon there.
2. Put the small amount of the butter in every ramekin.
3. Combine the salt, turmeric, and ground black pepper together. Mix it up.
4. Then shred Parmesan.
5. Chop the salmon and combine it with the spice mixture.
6. Place the chopped salmon in the bacon ramekins.
7. Add the cream and shredded cheese. Preheat the air fryer to 360 F.
8. Put the salmon boards in the air fryer basket and cook the dish for 10 minutes.
9. When the salmon boards are cooked – they will have little bit crunchy taste and light brown color.
10. Serve the dish only hot. Enjoy!

61. *Keto Tuna Pie*

Serves: 8 **Prep Time: 20 mins**

Cook Time: 30 mins

Calories: 156 **Carbs: 2.7g**

Protein: 8.8g **Fats: 20.3g**

Ingredients:

- ½ cup cream
- 1 ½ cup almond flour
- ½ teaspoon baking soda
- 1 tablespoon apple cider vinegar
- 1 onion, diced
- 1-pound Tuna
- 1 tablespoon chives
- 1 teaspoon dried oregano
- 1 teaspoon dried dill
- 1 teaspoon butter
- 1 egg
- 1 teaspoon dried parsley
- 1 teaspoon ground paprika

Directions:

1. Beat the egg in the bowl and whisk it. Then add the cream and keep whisking it for 2 minutes more.

2. After this, add baking soda and apple cider vinegar. Add almond flour and knead the smooth and non-sticky dough.
3. Then chop the Tuna into tiny pieces. Sprinkle the chopped Tuna with the diced onion, chives, dried oregano, dried dill, dried parsley, and ground paprika.
4. Mix the fish up. Then cut the dough into 2 parts. Cover the air fryer basket tray with the parchment.
5. Put the first part of the dough in the air fryer basket tray and make the crust from it with the help of the fingertips.
6. Then place the Tuna filling. Roll the second part of the dough with the help of the rolling pin and cover the Tuna filling. Secure the pie edges. Preheat the air fryer to 360 F.
7. Put the air fryer basket tray in the air fryer and cook the pie for 15 minutes.
8. After this, reduce the power to 355 F and cook the pie for 15 minutes more.
9. When the pie is cooked – remove it from the air fryer basket and chill little.
10. Slice the pie and serve. Enjoy!

62. *Turkey Quesadilla*

Serves: 2   **Prep Time: 5 mins.**

Cook Time: 5 mins

Calories: 414   **Carbs: 20g**

Protein: 29g   **Fats: 35g**

Ingredients:
- 1 tablespoon olive oil
- 2 low-carbohydrate tortillas
- ½ cup shredded Mexican blend cheese
- 2 ounces shredded turkey
- 2 tablespoons sour cream

Directions:
1. In a large skillet over medium-high heat, heat the olive oil.
2. Add a tortilla, then top with ¼ cup of cheese, the turkey, the Tajin seasoning, and the remaining ¼ cup of cheese. Top with the second tortilla.
3. Peek under the edge of the bottom tortilla to monitor how it is browning.
4. Once the bottom tortilla gets golden, and the cheese begins to melt, after about 2 minutes, flip the quesadilla over.
5. The second side will cook faster, about 1 minute.
6. Once the second tortilla is crispy and golden, transfer the quesadilla to a cutting board and let sit for 2 minutes.
7. Cut the quesadilla into 4 wedges using a pizza cutter or chef's knife.
8. Transfer half the quesadilla to each of two plates. Add 1 tablespoon of sour cream to each plate and serve hot.

63. *Buttery Garlic Turkey*

Serves: 2   **Prep Time: 5 mins.**

Cook Time: 40 mins

Calories: 642   **Carbs: 2g**

Protein: 57g   **Fats: 45g**

Ingredients:
- 2 tablespoons ghee melted
- 2 boneless skinless turkey breasts
- 4 tablespoons butter
- 2 garlic cloves minced
- ¼ cup grated Parmesan cheese

Directions:
1. Set your oven to preheat to 375 degrees F. Choose a baking dish that is large enough to hold both turkey breasts and coat it with the ghee.
2. Pat dry the turkey breasts and season with pink salt, pepper, and Italian seasoning. Place the turkey in the baking dish.
3. In a medium skillet over medium heat, melt the butter. Add the minced garlic and cook for about 5 minutes.
4. You want the garlic very lightly browned but not burned.
5. Remove the butter-garlic mixture from the heat and pour it over the turkey breasts.
6. Roast the turkey in the oven for 30 to 35 minutes, until cooked through.
7. Sprinkle some of the Parmesan cheese on top of each turkey breast.
8. Let the turkey rest in the baking dish for 5 minutes.
9. Divide the turkey between two plates, spoon the butter sauce over the turkey, and serve.

64. *Creamy Slow-Cooker Pork*

Serves: 2   **Prep Time: 10 mins.**

Cook Time: 4 hrs. 15 mins

Calories: 900   **Carbs: 9g**

Protein: 70g   **Fats: 66g**

Ingredients:
- 2 pork butts
- 1 cup Alfredo Sauce
- ¼ cup chopped sun-dried tomatoes
- ¼ cup grated Parmesan cheese
- 2 cups fresh spinach

Directions:
1. In a medium skillet over medium-high heat, melt the ghee.
2. Add the pork and cook, about 4 minutes on each side, until brown.
3. With the crock insert in place, transfer the pork to your slow cooker. Set your slow cooker to low.
4. In a small bowl, mix to combine the Alfredo sauce, sun-dried tomatoes, and Parmesan cheese, and season with pink salt and pepper. Pour the sauce over the pork.
5. Cover and cook on low for 4 hours, or until the pork is cooked through.
6. Add the fresh spinach. Cover and cook for 5 minutes more, until the spinach is slightly wilted, and serve.

☐

65. *Baked Garlic and Paprika Turkey Legs*

Serves: 2   **Prep Time: 10 mins.**

Cook Time: 55 mins

Calories: 700   **Carbs: 10g**

Protein: 63g   **Fats: 45g**

Ingredients:

- 1 lb. turkey legs
- 2 tablespoons paprika
- 2 garlic cloves minced
- ½ pound fresh green beans
- 1 tablespoon olive oil

Directions:

1. Set oven to 350°F.
2. Combine all your Ingredients in a large bowl, toss to combine and transfer to a baking dish.
3. Bake for 60 minutes until crisp and thoroughly cooked.

66. *Juicy Barbecue Ribs*

Serves: 2 **Prep Time: 10 mins.**

Cook Time: 4 hrs.

Calories: 956 **Carbs: 5g**

Protein: 68g **Fats: 72g**

Ingredients:

- 1lb. pork ribs
- Pink salt
- Freshly ground black pepper
- 1.25 oz. package dry rib-seasoning rub
- ½ cup sugar-free barbecue sauce

Directions:

1. With the crock insert in place, preheat your slow cooker to high.
2. Generously season the pork ribs with pink salt, pepper, and dry rib-seasoning rub.
3. Stand the ribs up along the walls of the slow-cooker insert, with the bonier side facing inward.
4. Pour the barbecue sauce on both sides of the ribs, using just enough to coat.
5. Cover, cook for 4 hours and serve.

▢▢

67. *Steak Bibimbap*

Serves: 2   **Prep Time: 10 mins.**

Cook Time: 15 mins.

Calories: 261   **Carbs: 2.6g**

Protein: 20.7g   **Fats: 17.5g**

Ingredients:

- 1 tablespoon ghee
- ½ pound ground beef, minced
- Pink salt
- Black pepper
- 1 tablespoon soy sauce

Directions:

1. In a large skillet over medium-high heat, heat the ghee.
2. Add the ground beef, and season with pink salt and pepper.
3. Use a wooden spoon, stir often, breaking the steak apart.
4. Stir while adding the soy sauce. Turn the heat to medium and simmer while you make the cauliflower rice and egg.

☐

68. *Sesame Pork and Bean Sprout*

Serves: 2   **Prep Time: 5 mins.**

Cook Time: 10 mins.

Calories: 366   **Carbs: 5g**

Protein: 33g   **Fats: 24g**

Ingredients:
- 2 boneless pork chops
- 2 tablespoons toasted sesame oil divided
- 2 tablespoons soy sauce
- 1 teaspoon Sriracha sauce
- 1 cup fresh bean sprout

Directions:
1. On a cutting board, pat the pork chops dry with a paper towel. Slice the chops into strips, and season to taste.
2. Set a skillet with a tablespoon of oil over medium heat.
3. Add the pork strips and cook them for 7 minutes, stirring occasionally.
4. In a small bowl, mix to combine the remaining 1 tablespoon of sesame oil, the soy sauce, and the Sriracha sauce. Pour into the skillet with the pork.
5. Add the bean sprout to the skillet, switch to low heat, and simmer for 3 to 5 minutes.
6. Divide the pork, bean sprout, and sauce between two wide, shallow bowls and serve.

69. *Beef Burgers with Sriracha Mayo*

Serves: 2　　　　　**Prep Time: 10 mins.**

Cook Time: 10 mins.

Calories: 575　　　　**Carbs: 2g**

Protein: 31g　　　　**Fats: 49g**

Ingredients:

- 12 ounces ground beef
- 2 scallions, white and green parts, thinly sliced
- 1 tablespoon toasted sesame oil
- 1 tablespoon Sriracha sauce
- 2 tablespoons mayonnaise

Directions:

1. Combine the ground beef with the scallions and sesame oil in a reasonably sized bowl then season to taste. Form the beef mixture into 2 patties.
2. Set a greased skillet over medium heat and allow to get hot
3. Once very hot, add the burger patties and cook until done, about 8 minutes, flipping halfway.
4. Meanwhile, in a small bowl, mix the Sriracha sauce and mayonnaise.
5. Transfer the burgers to a plate and let rest for at least 5 minutes.
6. Top the burgers with the Sriracha mayonnaise and serve.

Dessert

70.   *Coconut Chocolate Ice Pops*

Serves: 4   **Prep Time: 2 hrs. 5 mins**

Cook Time:0 mins

Calories: 193   **Carbs: 2g**

Protein: 2g   **Fats: 20g**

Ingredients:

- ½ (13.5-ounce) can coconut cream
- 2 teaspoons Swerve natural sweetener
- 2 tablespoons unsweetened cocoa powder
- 2 tablespoons sugar-free chocolate chips

Directions:

1.   In a food processor (or blender), mix together the coconut cream, sweetener, and unsweetened cocoa powder.

2.   Pour into ice pop molds and drop chocolate chips into each mold.

3.   Freeze for at least 2 hours before serving.

☐

☐

71. *Crustless Cheesecake Bites*

Serves: 4   **Prep Time: 3 hrs**

Cook Time: 30 mins

Calories: 169   **Carbs: 9g**

Protein: 5g   **Fats: 15g**

Ingredients:

- 4 ounces cream cheese, at room temperature
- ¼ cup sour cream
- 2 large eggs
- ⅓ cup Swerve natural sweetener
- ¼ teaspoon vanilla extract

Directions:

1. Preheat the oven to 350°F.
2. In a medium mixing bowl, use a hand mixer to beat the cream cheese, sour cream, eggs, sweetener, and vanilla until well mixed.
3. Place silicone liners (or cupcake paper liners) in the cups of a muffin tin.
4. Pour the cheesecake batter into the liners and bake for 30 minutes.
5. Refrigerate until completely cooled before serving, about 3 hours.

72. *Blueberry Cheesecake Mousse*

Serves: 2   **Prep Time: 1 hr 10 mins**

Cook Time: 0 mins

Calories: 221   **Carbs: 11g**

Protein: 4g   **Fats: 21g**

Ingredients:
- 4 ounces cream cheese, at room temperature
- 1 tablespoon heavy (whipping) cream
- 1 teaspoon Swerve natural sweetener
- 1 teaspoon vanilla extract
- 4 blueberries, sliced (fresh or frozen)

Directions:
1. Break up the cream cheese block into smaller pieces and distribute evenly in a food processor (or blender). Add the cream, sweetener, and vanilla.
2. Mix together on high. I usually stop and stir twice and scrape down the sides of the bowl with a small rubber scraper to make sure everything is mixed well.
3. Add the blueberries to the food processor and mix until combined.
4. Divide the blueberry cheesecake mixture between two small dishes, and chill for 1 hour before serving.

73. *Macadamia Chocolate Chip Bread*

Serves: 4   Prep Time: 15 mins

Cook Time:18 mins

Calories: 202   Carbs: 3g

Protein: 5g   Fats: 15g

Ingredients:
- 5 medium eggs
- 1 cup homemade macadamia butter
- ¼ cup coconut flour
- 2 tablespoons maple syrup
- ½ cup chocolate chips
- 2 teaspoons apple cider vinegar
- 1 tablespoon vanilla extract
- ½ teaspoon baking soda
- ½ teaspoon baking powder

Directions:

1. We will make macadamia butter first. Put 2 cups of macadamia nuts in a bowl and cover it with water.

2. Let the nuts absorb the water for about an hour. Rinse them well and then add them to a food processor or a blender.

3. Process them until you get a creamy consistency. Be patient as this might take some time. Turn your oven to 350 F.

4. Add 1 cup of macadamia butter you made to a bowl. You will probably make more than you need so that you can leave the rest in the fridge for future use.

5. Use a food processor or a blender and add eggs, baking powder, baking soda, coconut flour, vanilla extract, and apple cider vinegar to it.

6. Process everything until the ingredients are smooth and well-combined.

7. Add the chocolate chips to the mixture and use a spoon to stir them in.

8. Add the butter to the mixture and combine until you mix the ingredients well.

9. Pour the batter into the loaf pan and even the top out. Bake for about 30 minutes at 350F. Allow it to cool down a bit before serving.

74. *Coconut Cinnamon Bread*

Serves: 10 slice   **Prep Time: 15 mins**

Cook Time:30 mins

Calories: 80   **Carbs: 16g**

Protein: 2g   **Fats: 1g**

Ingredients:

- 3 eggs, pastured
- 1 tsp vinegar
- 3 tbsp butter, salted
- 2 tbsp water
- ½ cup coconut flour
- ½ tsp baking soda
- 1 tsp cinnamon
- ½ tsp baking powder
- pure sour cream/Greek Yogurt
- ⅛ tsp stevia or sweetener of choice

Directions:

1. Preheat the oven to 350 degrees F. Oil the loaf pan then lines the bottom with parchment paper.
2. Mix the dry ingredients using a whisk until well blended. Add the rest of the ingredients to the dry mixture and mix well.
3. Taste for sweetness and if needed, adjust. Let the mixture stand for 3 minutes then mix again.
4. Spread the batter onto the prepared loaf pan and bake for around 25-30 minutes until when you insert a toothpick at the center it comes out clean.
5. Cool the loaf on a wire rack then store in the refrigerator.

75.*Keto Almond Butter Bread*

Serves: 10   **Prep Time: 10 mins**

Cook Time:1 hr

Calories: 105   **Carbs: 4g**

Protein:5 g   **Fats: 15g**

Ingredients:
- 2 cups Almond flour
- 1/4 cup Psyllium husk powder
- 1 tbsp Baking powder, gluten-free)
- 1/2 tsp Salt
- 4 large Eggs, beaten
- 1/4 cup Almond Butter, melted
- 1/2 cup Warm water

Directions:
1. Set your oven to preheat to 350 degrees F, then prepare a loaf pan (9x5 preferably) by lining with parchment paper.
2. Add your salt, baking powder, psyllium husk powder, and almond flour to a large bowl, and stir.
3. Add in almond butter, eggs, and water then stir until just combined.
4. Pour batter in your prepared loaf pan and form a smooth round top (resembling your typical bread).
5. Set to bake until the top becomes hard and set to bake until the top becomes hard, and a toothpick can be inserted in the center and remain clean when removed (about 60 - 70 minutes).
6. Allow to cool fully before serving.

76. *Mini Keto Cream Donut*

Serves: 8   **Prep Time: 15 mins**

Cook Time:35 mins

Calories: 319   **Carbs: 3g**

Protein: 10g   **Fats: 17g**

Ingredients:
- 3 oz. of cream cheese
- 3 medium to large eggs
- 3 2/3 tablespoons of almond flour
- 1 ½ tablespoons of coconut flour
- 1 ½ teaspoons of coconut flour
- 1 teaspoon of baking powder
- Teaspoon of vanilla extract
- 4 teaspoons of erythritol extract
- 10 drops of stevia (liquid)

Directions:
1. With the aid of an immersion blender, gently mix and blend all the ingredients thoroughly, then heat the donut maker up and spray the inside with some coconut oil.
2. Pour the batter equally into the portions of the donut maker. Let the donut batter cook for about 3 minutes on one side and 3 minutes on the other side.
3. Remove the donuts from the donut maker and set the donuts aside to cool and repeat the procedure with the remaining batter if you can't finish them at once.

☐

77. *Caramel Frosted Banana Bread*

Serves: 10   **Prep Time: 30 mins**

Cook Time:1 hr. 15 mins

Calories: 202   **Carbs: 3g**

Protein: 5g   **Fats: 15g**

Ingredients:
- 1/3 cup coconut flour
- ½ cup chia seed, ground
- 2 cups almond flour
- 1/3 cup whey protein powder, unflavored
- ¾ cup almond milk, unsweetened
- ¼ cup butter, melted
- 3 big eggs
- 1 teaspoon banana extract
- 1 tablespoon baking powder
- ½ teaspoon vanilla extract
- ½ cup Swerve
- ¼ teaspoon stevia extract

Frosting:
- ¼ cup Swerve, powdered
- 4 ounces cream cheese
- 1 teaspoon caramel flavor
- 6 tablespoons whipping cream

Directions:

1. Turn your oven to 325 F. Use olive oil or butter to grease a loaf pan. Grab a bowl and add ground chia seed and water.
2. You can grind chia seeds in a coffee grinder. Let the mixture sit for about 30 minutes in order for the seeds to absorb the water.
3. Your goal is to get a consistency of mashed bananas. If needed, add more water.
4. Grab a big bowl and add coconut flour, almond flour, Swerve or another sweetener, whey protein powder, salt, and baking powder. Combine the ingredients well.
5. Add chia, almond milk, vanilla extract, banana extract, stevia extract, melted butter and eggs.
6. Stir the ingredients until you thoroughly combine them. Transfer the mixture to the loaf pan and even out the top.
7. Bake for around 70 minutes at 325 F or until the top becomes golden brown.
8. Make the frosting by combining powdered sweetener and softened cream cheese in a big bowl.
9. Next, add caramel flavor and whipping cream and continue beating until you combine the ingredients well.
10. Spread the frosting over the bread and allow it to cool down before serving.

78. *Keto Cinnamon Crunch*

Serves: 6   **Prep Time: 45 mins**

Cook Time:1 hr

Calories: 129   **Carbs: 2g**

Protein: 5g   **Fats: 9g**

Ingredients:
- ½ a cup of flax seed (milled)
- ½ a cup of hemp seeds (hulled)
- 2 tablespoons of ground cinnamon
- ½ a cup of apple juice
- 1 tablespoon of coconut oil

Directions:
1. Get a blender, magic bullet or food processor, then combine all the dry ingredient inside, then add the apple juice with the coconut oil and blend perfectly well until it has achieved a smooth consistency.
2. Put a parchment paper on cookie sheet and spread the batter on top press them down and make then thin in sizes.
3. Bake the batter in an oven that has been pre-heated to around 350-degree F, and for about 15 minutes.
4. Reduce the heat to around 250 degrees F and bake further for about 10 minutes.
5. With the aid of a knife or cutter for pizza, gently remove the baked crunch cereal from the oven and cut them into squares.
6. Turn on the oven back and put the crunch cereal back and bake further for about an hour until they become crispy and break easily (if they remain soft after baking for about an hour, simply return to the oven and bake until it is completely crispy and dried.
7. You may want to serve them with unsweetened almond or coconut milk.

79. *Cinnamon Bread*

Serves: 10   **Prep Time: 5 mins**

Cook Time:25 mins

Calories: 80   **Carbs: 1g**

Protein: 2g   **Fats: 16g**

Ingredients:
- 1/2 cup Coconut flour
- 1/2 tsp Baking soda
- 1/2 tsp Baking powder
- 1 tsp Cinnamon
- 1/8 tsp Stevia
- Eggs 3, pastured
- 1 tsp Vinegar
- 1/3 cup Sour cream, pure
- 3 tbsp Butter, salted
- 2 tbsp Water

Directions:
1. Set your oven to preheat to 350 degrees F and prepare a loaf tin (preferably 9x5) by lining with parchment paper.
2. Crack your eggs and add it to your food processor and pulse until fully beaten.
3. Add remaining ingredients to food processor and continue to pulse until your dough is formed.
4. Add dough to a loaf tin and set to bake until the top becomes hard and you can insert a toothpick, and it comes back out clean (about 60 - 70 minutes). Allow to cool fully, then serve.

80. _Blackberry Shake_

Serves: 2   **Prep Time: 10 mins**

Cook Time: 0 mins.

Calories: 407   **Carbs: 13g**

Protein: 4g   **Fats: 42g**

Ingredients:

- ¾ cup heavy, whipping cream
- 2 ounces cream cheese, at room temperature
- 1 tablespoon Swerve natural sweetener
- 6 blackberries, sliced
- 6 ice cubes

Directions:

1. Combine all your ingredients in your blender and process until smooth.
2. Pour into two tall glasses and serve.

81. Root Beer Float

Serves: 2   **Prep Time: 5 mins**

Cook Time: 0 mins.

Calories: 56   **Carbs: 3g**

Protein: 1g   **Fats: 6g**

Ingredients:

- 1, 12-ounce can diet root beer
- 4 tablespoons heavy, whipping cream
- 1 teaspoon vanilla extract
- 6 ice cubes

Directions:

1. Combine all your ingredients in your blender and process until smooth.
2. Pour into two tall glasses and serve.

☐

82. *Mixed Berries Cheesecake Fat Bomb*

Serves: 2   **Prep Time: 2hrs. 10 mins**

Cook Time: 0 mins.

Calories: 414   **Carbs: 9g**

Protein: 4g   **Fats: 43g**

Ingredients:

- 4 ounces cream cheese, room temperature
- 2 teaspoons Swerve natural sweetener
- 4 tablespoons, ½ stick butter, room temperature
- 1 teaspoon vanilla extract
- ¼ cup mix berries, fresh or frozen

Directions:

1. In a medium bowl, use a hand mixer to beat the cream cheese, butter, sweetener, and vanilla.
2. In a small bowl, mash the berries thoroughly. Fold the berries into the cream-cheese mixture using a rubber scraper.
3. Spoon the cream-cheese mixture into fat bomb molds.
4. Freeze for at least 2 hours, unmold them, and eat!
5. Leftover fat bombs can be stored in the freezer in a zip-top bag for up to 3 months.
6. It's nice to have some in your freezer for when you are craving a sweet treat.

83. *Almond Fat Bombs*

Serves: 12   **Prep Time: 25 mins + freezing time**
Cook Time: 5 mins
Calories: 120   **Carbs: 2g**
Protein: 0.9g   **Fats: 14.4g**

Ingredients:
- 5 tablespoon swerve
- 6 tablespoon almond butter
- ½ teaspoon vanilla extract
- ¼ teaspoon salt
- 6 tablespoon Erythritol
- 1 teaspoon stevia extract
- 8 tablespoon fresh lemon juice
- 3 eggs
- 1 teaspoon lime zest
- 2 tablespoon coconut oil

Directions:
1. Set your almond butter on to melt. Stir in your swerve once melted then whisk in your salt, vanilla extract, and Erythritol.
2. Transfer your mixture to your truffle mold then set to freeze.
3. While that goes, combine your coconut oil, stevia extract, lime zest and lemon juice then whisk well.
4. Whip your eggs and lemon mixture together using a hand mixer until smooth.
5. Set a deep pot on to boil then top with a metal mixing bowl to create a double boiler. Be sure that the mixing bowl does not touch the liquid.
6. Reduce to a simmer and pour your egg mixture into the mixing bowl, whisking continuously until curd it cooked (about 5 minutes). Remove from heat and set to chill.
7. Place the cooled curd into a piping bag then use it to stuff your fat bombs. Enjoy!

84. *Cocoa Fat Bombs*

Serves: 15   **Prep Time: 10 mins**
Cook Time: 5 mins
Calories: 130   **Carbs: 2.7g**
Protein: 0.9g   **Fats: 14.4g**

Ingredients:
- 1/2 cup coconut butter
- 1/4 cup extra virgin coconut oil
- 1/2 cup butter or more coconut oil
- 3 tbs unsweetened cocoa powder
- 15 to 20 drops liquid stevia
- Optional: 2 tbs erythritol or Swerve, powdered
- Optional: 1 tsp cherry, hazelnut, or almond extract, or pinch of cayenne
- pepper

Directions:
1. Let the coconut butter, coconut oil, and butter sit at room temperature to soften, but do not let melt.
2. In a food processor, combine all the ingredients but keep some cocoa aside for coating. Process until smooth.
3. Place a parchment paper and line it into a baking sheet. Use a spoon to form 15 small truffles. Place in the fridge for 30 to 60 minutes.
4. Remove the bomb from the fridge and sift the rest of the cacao powder over it.
5. Preheat your Air Fryer to 350 degrees F. Place the bombs in the Air Fryer basket with some space between each and let it cook for 5 minutes.
6. Cool to room temperature then store in the fridge for up to a week or freeze for up to three months.

85. *Hot Chocolate Fat Bombs*

Serves: 15   **Prep Time: 10 mins**

Cook Time: 5 mins

Calories: 145   **Carbs: 4.8g**

Protein: 0.9g   **Fats: 14.4g**

Ingredients:

- 1/4 cup extra virgin coconut oil
- 1/2 cup butter or more coconut oil
- 3 tablespoons unsweetened chocolate powder
- 15 to 20 drops liquid stevia
- Optional: 2 tablespoons erythritol or Swerve, powdered
- Optional: 1 teaspoon cherry, hazelnut, or almond extract, or pinch of cayenne pepper
- 1/2 cup coconut butter

Directions:

1. Let the coconut butter, coconut oil, and butter sit at room temperature to soften, but do not let melt.
2. In a food processor, combine all the ingredients but keep some cocoa aside for coating. Process until smooth.
3. Place a parchment paper and line it into a baking sheet. Use a spoon to form 15 small truffles. Place in the fridge for 30 to 60 minutes.
4. Remove the bomb from the fridge and sift the rest of the cacao powder over it.
5. Preheat your Air Fryer to 350 degrees F. Place the bombs in the Air Fryer basket with some space between each and let it cook for 5 minutes.
6. Cool to room temperature then store in the fridge for up to a week or freeze for up to three months.

86. *Peanut Fat Bombs*

Serves: 12　　　　**Prep Time: 25 mins + freezing time**
Cook Time: 5 mins
Calories: 134　　　　**Carbs: 2.7g**
Protein: 0.9g　　　　**Fats: 14.4g**

Ingredients:
- 5 tablespoon swerve
- 6 tablespoon peanut butter
- ½ teaspoon vanilla extract
- ¼ teaspoon salt
- 6 tablespoon Erythritol
- 1 teaspoon stevia extract
- 8 tablespoon fresh lemon juice
- 3 eggs
- 1 teaspoon lime zest
- 2 tablespoon coconut oil

Directions:
1. Set your peanut butter on to melt. Stir in your swerve once melted then whisk in your salt, vanilla extract, and Erythritol.
2. Transfer your mixture to your truffle mold then set to freeze.
3. While that goes, combine your coconut oil, stevia extract, lime zest and lemon juice then whisk well.
4. Whip your eggs and lemon mixture together using a hand mixer until smooth.
5. Set a deep pot on to boil then top with a metal mixing bowl to create a double boiler. Be sure that the mixing bowl does not touch the liquid.
6. Reduce to a simmer and pour your egg mixture into the mixing bowl, whisking continuously until curd it cooked (about 5 minutes). Remove from heat and set to chill.
7. Place the cooled curd into a piping bag then use it to stuff your fat bombs. Enjoy!

87. *Strawberry Ketogenic Scones*

Serves: 10   **Prep Time: 10 mins**

Cook Time: 20 mins

Calories: 154   **Carbs: 6g**

Protein: 7g   **Fats: 12.5g**

Ingredients:

- 2 Cups of almond flour
- 1/3 Cup of Swerve Sweetener
- ¼ Cup of coconut flour
- 1 tbsp of baking powder
- ¼ tsp of salt
- 2 Eggs
- ¼ Cup of heavy whipping cream
- ½ tsp of vanilla extract
- ¾ Cup of fresh strawberries

Directions:

1. Preheat your Air Fryer to a temperature of about 325° F and line your Air Fryer pan with a parchment paper.
2. Combine your salt, almond flour, coconut flour, baking powder and sweetener.
3. Add in your vanilla, eggs, and whipping cream; mold into a dough. Add in the strawberries and gently whisk.
4. Roll out the dough then cut into triangles. Transfer to your lined air fryer pan then set to fry at 340 F for about 20 minutes.
5. When the timer beeps, turn off your Air Fryer; then let the cones cool for about 5 minutes. Serve and enjoy your scones!

88. *Blueberry Coconut Brownies*

Serves: 6-7   **Prep Time: 10 mins**

Cook Time: 20 mins

Calories: 183.5   **Carbs: 4.8g**

Protein: 3g   **Fats: 16.9g**

Ingredients:

- softened butter, 1½ cups
- granulated stevia, 4 tbsp
- unsweetened cocoa powder, ½ Cup
- eggs, 2, Medium
- vanilla, 1 tsp
- coconut, 1 cup, unsweetened, shredded
- almond flour, 1 cup
- baking powder, ½ tsp
- blueberries, 1 cup

Directions:

1. Whisk together your butter and sweetener until fully creamed.
2. Fold in the remaining ingredients then pour into a lightly greased baking pan.
3. Set to air fry at 355 F for about 20 minutes.
4. When done, slice into squares then serve. Enjoy!

89. *Ginger Biscotti*

Serves: 6-7　　　**Prep Time: 10 mins**
Cook Time: 20 mins
Calories: 152　　　**Carbs: 4.5g**
Protein: 6.9g　　　**Fats: 16.9g**

Ingredients:

- 2 Cups of whole almonds
- 2 tbsp of chia seeds
- ¼ Cup of coconut oil
- 1 Large egg
- 3 tbsp of freshly grated ginger
- 2 tbsp of cinnamon powder
- ½ tsp of nutmeg
- A quantity of stevia
- 1 Pinch of salt

Directions:

1. Preheat your Air Fryer to 175° C/ 350°F. Process the almonds with the ginger and the chia seeds.
2. Mix your ingredients together in a bowl. Line your Air Fryer pan with a cooking sheet.
3. Form small biscuits and arrange it over your baking sheet. Place the pan in your Air Fryer and lock the lid.
4. Set the timer to about 15 minutes and set the temperature to about 350° F.
5. When the timer beeps; turn off your Air Fryer.
6. Set the biscotti aside to cool for about 10 minutes. Serve and enjoy your biscotti!

90. *Hemp Cocoa Chocolate Fudge*

Serves: 2   **Prep Time: 10 mins**

Cook Time: 20 mins

Calories: 173   **Carbs: 5.2g**

Protein: 5g   **Fats: 9g**

Ingredients:
- 2 tbsp of unflavored hemp protein powder
- 1 tbsp of cocoa powder
- ¼ Cup of egg whites
- 1 tbsp of melted coconut oil
- 2 tsp of birch-sourced xylitol
- 2 tbsp of dairy-free divided chocolate chips

Directions:
1. Preheat your Air Fryer to a temperature of about 185°C/ 375°F.
2. Combine all your ingredients except for the chocolate chips in a mixing bowl
3. Pour the mixture in a steel ramekin or a heat proof ramekin.
4. Top the ramekin with the chocolate chips.
5. Put the ramekin in your Air Fryer basket and lock the lid.
6. Set the temperature to about 375° F and set the timer to about 20 minutes.
7. When the timer beeps; turn off your Air Fryer and set the ramekin aside to cool for 5 minutes.
8. Serve and enjoy your delicious dessert!

Bread

91. Coconut Flax Bread

Serves: 10   **Prep Time: 10 mins.**
Cook Time: 45 mins
Calories:143.9   **Protein: 6.3g**
Carbs: 5.1g   **Fat: 12.2g**

Ingredients:
- Coconut flour, 1 1/2 cups
- Flax seeds, 1/4 cup ground
- Flax seeds, 1 tbsp., whole
- Salt, 1/2 tsp.
- Baking soda, 1/2 tsp.
- Eggs, 4, pastured, beaten
- Honey, 2 tsp.
- Apple cider vinegar, 1/2 tsp.
- Butter, 1 tsp., for greasing

Directions:
1. Set your oven to preheat to 300 degrees F, and lightly grease a loaf tin with butter, then set aside.
2. Add all your ingredients to a large bowl and stir to combine.
3. Pour batter into loaf tin and set to bake until the top becomes hard and you can insert a toothpick, and it comes back out clean, about 45 minutes.
4. Allow to cool fully, serve, and enjoy.

92. *Cauliflower and Almond Flour Bread*

Serves: 10   **Prep Time: 10 mins.**
Cook Time: 30 mins
Calories:108   **Protein: 6g**
Carbs: 3g   Fat: 8g

Ingredients:
- Cauliflower, 1 small head, chopped, roasted
- Olive oil, 1/4 cup, extra virgin
- Almond milk, 1/4 cup, unsweetened
- Eggs, 6
- Almond flour, 3/4 cup
- Baking soda, 1/2 tsp.
- Salt, 1/2 tsp.
- Garlic powder, 1 tsp.

Directions:

Set your oven to preheat to 350 degrees F, and lightly grease a loaf tin with butter, then set aside.

Add all your ingredients to a large bowl and stir to combine.

Pour batter into loaf tin and set to bake until the top becomes hard and you can insert a toothpick, and it comes back out clean, about 30 minutes.

Allow to cool fully, then serve.

93. *Whey Keto Bread*

Serves: 6   **Prep Time: 20 mins.**

Cook Time: 30 mins

Calories:99   **Protein: 4.28g**

Carbs: 2.42g   **Fat: 8.51g**

Ingredients:

- Eggs, 12, separated
- Whey protein, 1 cup
- Onion powder, ½ tsp

Directions:

1. Set your oven to preheat to 325 degrees F and prepare a loaf tin, preferably 9x5 by lining with parchment paper.
2. Crack your eggs and add it to your food processor then pulse until stiff peaks form.
3. Add remaining ingredients to food processor and continue to pulse until your dough is formed.
4. Add dough to a loaf tin and set to bake until the top becomes hard and you can insert a toothpick, and it comes back out clean, about 30 minutes.
5. Allow to cool fully, then serve.

94. *Keto Focaccia Bread*

Serves: 12   **Prep Time: 15 mins.**

Cook Time: 20 mins.

Calories:80.4   **Protein: 3.3g**

Carbs: 3.2g   **Fat: 6.8g**

Ingredients:
- flax seed meal, 2 cups
- baking powder, 1 tbsp.
- salt, 1 tsp.
- sugar, 2 tbsp.
- eggs, 5, beaten
- water, ½ cup
- oil, ⅓ cup

Directions:
1. Set your oven to preheat to 350 degrees F and prepare a loaf tin, preferably 9x5 by lining with parchment paper.
2. Crack your eggs and add it to your food processor and pulse until fully beaten.
3. Add remaining ingredients to food processor and continue to pulse until your dough is formed.
4. Add dough to a loaf tin and set to bake until the top becomes hard and you can insert a toothpick and it comes back out clean, about 28 minutes.
5. Allow to cool fully then serve.

95. *Almond Breadsticks*

Serves: 6   **Prep Time: 10 mins.**
Cook Time: 20 mins.
Calories: 100   **Protein: 8.4g**
Carbs: 3g   **Fat: 14.2g**

Ingredients:
- Bread stick base
- 2 cups mozzarella cheese
- 1 tablespoon Psyllium husk powder
- 1 large egg
- 1 teaspoon baking powder
- 3 tablespoons cream cheese
- ¾ cup almond flour
- Extra cheesy
- 1 teaspoon onion powder
- 1 teaspoon garlic powder
- 1/4 cup parmesan cheese
- 3 oz. cheddar cheese
- Italian style
- 1 teaspoon salt
- 2 tablespoons Italian seasoning
- 1 teaspoon pepper
- Cinnamon sweet
- 3 tablespoons butter
- 2 tablespoons cinnamon
- 6 tablespoons swerve sweetener

Directions:
1. Preheat the oven to 400 degrees F. Mix the cream cheese and the egg until slightly combined then set aside.

2. Combine all the dry ingredients.
3. Set your mozzarella cheese to melt using 20 seconds intervals in the microwave, stirring between each interval until sizzling.
4. Add in your eggs, cream cheese, and dry ingredients in with your mozzarella.
5. Knead to create a dough then set on a non-stick mat.
6. Press the dough flat until the baking sheet is totally covered with dough.
7. Transfer the dough to a foil using a pizza cutter to slice it.

Note: never use sharp objects and knives on a non-stick mat. Cut the dough then season as per the ingredient mentioned above. Bake for around 13-15 minutes on the top rack until crisp. Serve while warm with marinara or cream cheese butter cream, optional.

96. *Garlic Breadsticks*

Serves: 8   **Prep Time: 30 mins.**
Cook Time: 20 mins.
Calories: 259.2   **Protein: 7g**
Carbs: 6.3g   **Fat: 24.7g**

Ingredients:
Garlic butter:
- 1/4 cup Butter, softened
- 1 tsp Garlic Powder

Breadsticks:
- 2 cup Almond Flour
- 1/2 Tbsp Baking Powder
- 1 Tbsp Psyllium Husk Powder
- 1/4 tsp Salt
- 3 Tbsp Butter, melted
- 1 Egg
- 1/4 cup Boiling Water

Directions:
1. Heat your oven to 400F / 200C. Line your baking sheet with parchment paper and set aside.
2. Beat the butter with the garlic powder and set aside to use it for brushing.
3. Combine the almond flour, salt, baking powder and psyllium husk powder.
4. Add the butter along with the egg and mix until well combined.
5. Pour in the boiling water and mix until dough forms. Divide the dough into 8 equal pieces and roll them into breadsticks.
6. Place dough on baking sheet, allow to bake for 15 minutes. Brush the breadsticks with the garlic butter and bake for 5 more minutes. Serve warm or allow to cool.

97. *Cheesy Cauliflower Bread Sticks*

Serves: 2   **Prep Time: 15 mins.**

Cook Time: 45 mins.

Calories: 108   **Protein: 10g**

Carbs: 6g   **Fat: 24g**

Ingredients:

- 1 cup shredded mozzarella cheese
- 1 tablespoon organic butter
- 1 egg
- 1/2 teaspoon Italian seasoning
- 1/4 teaspoon red pepper flakes
- 1/8 teaspoon kosher salt
- 2 cups diced cauliflower, cooked for 3 minutes in the microwave
- 3 teaspoons minced garlic
- Parmesan cheese, the grated / powdered kind

Directions:

1. Preheat oven to 350 degrees F. Place the butter in a small pan and melt over low heat.
2. Add the red pepper flakes and garlic to the butter and cook for 2-3 minutes over low heat; don't let the butter brown.
3. Add the garlic and butter mixture to the bowl with the cooked cauliflower then add the Italian seasoning and salt to the bowl and mix.
4. Refrigerate for 10 minutes then add the mozzarella cheese and eggs to the bowl and mix.
5. Place a layer of parchment paper at the bottom of your 9×9 baking dish and grease with cooking spray or butter.
6. Add the egg and mozzarella to the cauliflower mixture. Add mixture to pan and smooth to a thin layer with your palms.
7. Bake for 30 minutes then take out of oven and top with some few shakes of parmesan and mozzarella cheese.
8. Cook for 8 more minutes then remove from oven and cut into sticks. Enjoy

98. *Spicy Parmesan Breadsticks*

Serves: 5   **Prep Time: 20 mins.**
Cook Time: 15 mins.
Calories: 100   **Protein: 8.4g**
Carbs: 3g   **Fat: 14.2g**

Ingredients:
- raw cauliflower, 1 head, riced
- mozzarella cheese, ½ cup, shredded
- egg, 1 large
- black pepper, 2 tsps., ground
- salt, 1 tsp.
- parmesan cheese, ½ cup, shaved
- basil, ½ tbsp., freshly chopped
- parsley, ½ tbsp., freshly chopped Italian flat-leaf
- mozzarella cheese, ¾ cup, shredded
- garlic, ½ tbsp., 1/2 freshly minced

Directions:
1. Heat oven to 425 degrees F. Use a silicone baking mat or parchment paper to line baking sheet.
2. Mix ½ teaspoon black pepper, 1 teaspoon salt, ½ tablespoon fresh parsley, ½ tablespoon fresh basil, ½ tablespoon garlic, 1 egg, ½ cup parmesan cheese, ½ cup shredded mozzarella cheese and riced cauliflower in a suitable size bowl until combined and held together.
3. Place the above mixture to the lined baking sheet then spread it out to form a rectangle about 9x7" and 1/4" thick.
4. Bake in the oven for around 10-12 minutes then remove and top with ¾ cup of the shredded mozzarella cheese.
5. Return to the oven and bake until the cheese melts and the bread begins to brown.
6. Leave it cool for about 10 minutes then slice into breadsticks. Garnish with parmesan cheese and fresh herbs.
7. Serve with your preferred red sauce and enjoy.

99. *Cinnamon Swirl Bread*

Serves: 10   **Prep Time: 10 mins.**
Cook Time: 40 mins
Calories:90   **Protein: 4g**
Carbs: 2.5g   **Fat: 14g**

Ingredients:

- Sunflower seed butter, 1 cup
- Coconut palm sugar, 1/4 cup
- Eggs, 3
- Vinegar, 1 tbsp.
- Baking soda, 1/2 tsp.
- Salt, 1/4 tsp
- Stevia, 2 tbsp.
- Cinnamon, 1 tbsp.

Directions:

1. Set your oven to preheat to 355 degrees F and prepare a loaf tin, preferably 9x5 by lining with parchment paper.
2. Crack your eggs and add it to your food processor and pulse until fully beaten.
3. Add remaining ingredients, except stevia, and cinnamon, to food processor and continue to pulse until your dough is formed.
4. Add dough to a loaf tin, and sprinkle stevia and cinnamon on top.
5. Stick a knife directly in the dough and turn to create swirls throughout the dough.
6. Set to bake until the top becomes hard and you can insert a toothpick, and it comes back out clean, about 40 minutes. Allow to cool fully then serve.

100. *Nutty Garlic Bread*

Serves: 10   **Prep Time: 15 mins.**
Cook Time: 25 mins.
Calories:180   **Protein: 11g**
Carbs: 4g   **Fat: 17g**

Ingredients:
Bread Base:
- Almond flour, 1 1/4 cups
- Coconut flour, 1 tbsp.
- Egg whites, 3, beaten well
- Olive oil, 2 tbsp.
- Warm water, 1/4 cup
- Yeast granules, 1 tsp., live
- Coconut sugar, 1 tsp.
- Mozzarella cheese, 1/2 cup, shredded
- Salt, 1/4 tsp.
- Baking powder, 2 tsp.
- Garlic powder, 1/4 tsp.
- Xanthan, 1/2 tsp.

Topping:
- Mozzarella cheese, 1 cup, shredded
- Butter, 2 tbsp., melted
- Garlic powder, 1/4 tsp.
- Salt, 1/4 tsp.
- Italian seasoning, 1/2 tsp.

Directions:
1. Set your oven to preheat to 400 degrees F and prepare a loaf tin, preferably 9x5 by lining with parchment paper.

2. Crack your eggs and add it to your food processor and pulse until fully beaten.

3. Add remaining ingredients, except topping ingredients, to food processor and continue to pulse until your dough is formed.

4. Add dough to a loaf tin and set to bake for 17 - 20 minutes or until the crust gets golden.

5. Add the topping ingredients and bake for another 17 - 20 minutes or until the top becomes hard and the cheese melts. Serve.

101. *Coconut Raisin Bread*

Serves: 18   **Prep Time: 10 mins.**

Cook Time: 1 hour

Calories:130.6   **Protein: 4.2g**

Carbs: 2.8g   **Fat: 22.2g**

Ingredients:

- Coconut flour, 2 cups
- Raisins, 1 cups
- Psyllium husk powder, 1/4 cup
- Baking powder, 1 tbsp., gluten-free
- Salt, 1/2 tsp
- Eggs, 4 large, beaten
- Coconut oil, 1/4 cup, melted
- Warm water, 1/2 cup

Directions:

1. Set your oven to preheat to 350 degrees F, then prepare a loaf pan, 9x5 preferably by lining with parchment paper.
2. Add your salt, psyllium husk powder, coconut flour and baking powder to a large bowl, and stir.
3. Add in coconut oil, eggs, and water then stir until just combined.
4. Pour batter in your prepared loaf pan and form a smooth round top, resembling your typical bread.
5. Set to bake until the top becomes hard and you can insert a toothpick, and it comes back out clean, about 60 - 70 minutes. Allow to cool fully then serve.

Conclusion

Thank you so much for taking the time to read and utilize the Keto for Women over 50 2021. I sincerely hope you were able to find value in what you read through and that these starter recipes were able to catapult you further along your keto journey.

I would love to hear your thought or feedback of the book. Please take a few minutes to leave me a review on Amazon or platform on which you made your purchase to share your thoughts or view on this keto guide.

Thank you again, and good luck on the remainder of your keto journey.

Printed in Great Britain
by Amazon

60211068R00087